W9-BZM-697

THE COMMUNIST MANIFESTO

KARL MARX
FREDERICK ENGELS

The
**COMMUNIST
MANIFESTO**

Pathfinder

NEW YORK   LONDON   MONTREAL   SYDNEY

COVER: From the Pathfinder Mural in New York City. In the *Communist Manifesto*, Marx and Engels point to the victory of the working class in England earlier in 1847 in gaining passage of the Ten-Hours Bill, which limited the hours of work of women and children. Over the next several decades, the international labor movement took up the struggle for an eight-hour day for the entire working class, a fight prominently featured in this detail from the mural.

COVER DESIGN: *Eva Braiman and Tom Tomasko*

Copyright © 1987, 2008 by Pathfinder Press.
All rights reserved

ISBN 978-1-60488-003-8
Library of Congress Control Number 2008930039

Manufactured in Canada

First Pathfinder edition, 1970
Second edition, 1987
Third edition, 2008
Eighth printing, 2020

PATHFINDER
www.pathfinderpress.com
pathfinder@pathfinderpress.com

CONTENTS

The History of the Russian Revolution

LEON TROTSKY

How, under Lenin's leadership, the Bolshevik Party led millions of workers and farmers to overthrow the state power of the landlords and capitalists in 1917 and bring to power a government that advanced their class interests at home and worldwide. Unabridged, 3 vols. in one. Written by one of the central leaders of that socialist revolution. $30. Also in French and Russian.

To See the Dawn

Baku, 1920—First Congress of the Peoples of the East

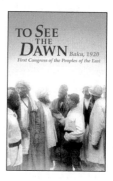

How can peasants and workers in the colonial world achieve freedom from imperialist exploitation? By what means can working people overcome divisions incited by their national ruling classes and act together for their common class interests? These questions were addressed by 2,000 delegates to the 1920 Congress of the Peoples of the East. $17

The Revolution Betrayed

What Is the Soviet Union and Where Is It Going?

LEON TROTSKY

In 1917 workers and peasants of Russia were the motor force for one of the deepest revolutions in history. Yet within ten years a political counterrevolution by a privileged social layer whose chief spokesperson was Joseph Stalin was being consolidated. The classic study of the Soviet workers state and its degeneration. $17. Also in Spanish, Farsi, and Greek.

PATHFINDER AROUND THE WORLD

Visit our website for a complete list of titles and to place orders

www.pathfinderpress.com

PATHFINDER DISTRIBUTORS

UNITED STATES
(and Caribbean, Latin America, and East Asia)
> *Pathfinder Books, 306 W. 37th St., 13th Floor*
> *New York, NY 10018*

CANADA
> *Pathfinder Books, 7107 St. Denis, Suite 204*
> *Montreal, QC H2S 2S5*

UNITED KINGDOM
(and Europe, Africa, Middle East, and South Asia)
> *Pathfinder Books, 5 Norman Rd.*
> *Seven Sisters, London N15 4ND*

AUSTRALIA
(and Southeast Asia and the Pacific)
> *Pathfinder Books, Suite 22, 10 Bridge St.*
> *Granville, Sydney, NSW 2142*

NEW ZEALAND
> *Pathfinder Books, 188a Onehunga Mall Rd., Onehunga, Auckland 1061*
> *Postal address: P.O. Box 13857, Auckland 1643*

PATHFINDER READERS CLUB • CLUB DE LECTORES

NAME
NOMBRE

EXPIRATION DATE • FECHA QUE VENCE: ___/___/___

Valid at Pathfinder book centers and online
Válido en centros de libros Pathfinder y en línea
www.pathfinderpress.com

Join the Pathfinder Readers Club
to get 25% discounts on all Pathfinder
titles and bigger discounts
on special offers.
Sign up at www.pathfinderpress.com
or through the distributors above.
$10 a year

Introduction

BY LEON TROTSKY

OCTOBER 1937

IT IS HARD TO BELIEVE that the centennial of the *Manifesto of the Communist Party* is only ten years away! This pamphlet, displaying greater genius than any other in world literature, astounds us even today by its freshness. Its most important sections appear to have been written yesterday. Assuredly, the young authors (Marx was twenty-nine, Engels twenty-seven) were able to look further into the future than anyone before them, and perhaps than anyone since them.

Already in their joint preface to the edition of 1872, Marx and Engels declared that despite the fact that certain secondary passages in the Manifesto were antiquated, they felt that they no longer had any right to alter the original text inasmuch as the Manifesto had already become a historical document, during the intervening period of twenty-five years. Sixty-five additional years have elapsed since that time. Isolated passages in the Manifesto have receded still further into the past. We shall try to establish succinctly in this preface both those ideas in the Manifesto which retain their full force today and those which require impor-

---

This introduction to the first edition of the Manifesto in Afrikaans was published originally in English under the title "Ninety Years of the Communist Manifesto," in *New International*, February 1938.

tant alteration or amplification.

1. The materialist conception of history, discovered by Marx only a short while before and applied with consummate skill in the Manifesto, has completely withstood the test of events and the blows of hostile criticism. It constitutes today one of the most precious instruments of human thought. All other interpretations of the historical process have lost all scientific meaning. We can state with certainty that it is impossible in our time to be not only a revolutionary militant but even a literate observer in politics without assimilating the materialist interpretation of history.

2. The first chapter of the Manifesto opens with the following words: "The history of all hitherto existing society is the history of class struggles." This postulate, the most important conclusion drawn from the materialist interpretation of history, immediately became an issue in the class struggle. Especially venomous attacks were directed by reactionary hypocrites, liberal doctrinaires, and idealistic democrats against the theory which replaced "common welfare," "national unity," and "eternal moral truths" as the driving force by the struggle of material interests. They were later joined by recruits from the ranks of the labor movement itself, by the so-called revisionists, i.e., the proponents of reviewing ("revising") Marxism in the spirit of class collaboration and class conciliation. Finally, in our own time, the same path has been followed in practice by the contemptible epigones of the Communist International (the "Stalinists"): the policy of the so-called People's Front flows wholly from the denial of the laws of the class struggle.[1] Meanwhile, it is precisely the epoch of imperialism, bringing all social contradictions to the point of highest tension, which gives to the *Communist Manifesto*

its supreme *theoretical* triumph.

3. The anatomy of capitalism, as a specific stage in the economic development of society, was given by Marx in its finished form in *Capital* (1867). But already in the *Communist Manifesto* the main lines of the future analysis are firmly sketched: the payment for labor power as equivalent to the cost of its reproduction; the appropriation of surplus value by the capitalists; competition as the basic law of social relations; the ruination of intermediate classes, i.e., the urban petty bourgeoisie and the peasantry; the concentration of wealth in the hands of an ever diminishing number of property owners at the one pole, and the numerical growth of the proletariat at the other; the preparation of the material and political preconditions for the socialist regime.

4. The proposition in the Manifesto condemning the tendency of capitalism to lower the living standards of the workers, and even to transform them into paupers, had been subjected to a heavy barrage. Parsons, professors, ministers, journalists, social democratic theoreticians, and trade union leaders came to the front against the so-called theory of impoverishment. They invariably discovered signs of growing prosperity among the toilers, palming off the labor aristocracy as the proletariat or taking a fleeting tendency as permanent. Meanwhile, even the development of the mightiest capitalism in the world, namely, U.S. capitalism, has transformed millions of workers into paupers who are maintained at the expense of federal, municipal, or private charity.

5. As against the Manifesto, which depicted commercial and industrial crises as a series of ever more extensive catastrophes, the revisionists vowed that the national

and international development of trusts would assure control over the market and lead gradually to the abolition of crises. The close of the last century and the beginning of the present one were in reality marked by a development of capitalism so tempestuous as to make crises seem only "accidental" stoppages. But this epoch has gone beyond return. In the last analysis, truth proved to be on Marx's side in this question as well.

6. "The executive of the modern state is but a committee for managing the common affairs of the whole bourgeoisie." This succinct formula, which the leaders of the social democracy looked upon as a journalistic paradox, contains in fact the only scientific theory of the state. The democracy fashioned by the bourgeoisie is not, as both Bernstein and Kautsky thought,[2] an empty sack which one can undisturbedly fill with any kind of class content. Bourgeois democracy can serve only the bourgeoisie. A government of the "People's Front," whether headed by Blum or Chautemps, Caballero or Negrín, is only "a committee for managing the common affairs of the whole bourgeoisie."[3] Whenever this "committee" manages affairs poorly, the bourgeoisie dismisses it with a boot.

7. "Every class struggle is a political struggle." "This organization of the proletarians into a class [is] consequently [its organization] into a political party." Trade unionists, on the one hand, and anarcho-syndicalists, on the other, have long shied away—and even now try to shy away—from the understanding of these historical laws. "Pure" trade unionism has now been dealt a crushing blow in its chief refuge: the United States. Anarcho-syndicalism has suffered an irreparable defeat in its last stronghold: Spain. Here too the Manifesto proved correct.

8. The proletariat cannot conquer power within the legal framework established by the bourgeoisie. Communists "openly declare that their ends can be attained only by the forcible overthrow of all existing social conditions." Reformism sought to explain this postulate of the Manifesto on the grounds of the immaturity of the movement at that time and the inadequate development of democracy. The fate of Italian, German, and a great number of other "democracies" proves that "immaturity" is the distinguishing trait of the ideas of the reformists themselves.

9. For the socialist transformation of society, the working class must concentrate in its hands such power as can smash each and every political obstacle barring the road to the new system. "The proletariat organized as the ruling class"—this is the dictatorship. At the same time it is the only true proletarian democracy. Its scope and depth depend upon concrete historical conditions. The greater the number of states that take the path of the socialist revolution, the freer and more flexible forms will the dictatorship assume, the broader and more deep-going will be workers democracy.

10. The international development of capitalism has predetermined the international character of the proletarian revolution. "United action, of the leading civilized countries at least, is one of the first conditions for the emancipation of the proletariat." The subsequent development of capitalism has so closely knit all sections of our planet, both "civilized" and "uncivilized," that the problem of the socialist revolution has completely and decisively assumed a world character. The Soviet bureaucracy attempted to liquidate the Manifesto with respect to this fundamental question. The Bonapartist degeneration of the Soviet state is an over-

whelming illustration of the falseness of the theory of socialism in one country.[4]

11. "When, in the course of development, class distinctions have disappeared, and all production has been concentrated in the hands of a vast association of the whole nation, the public power will lose its political character." In other words: the state withers away. Society remains, freed from the straitjacket. This is nothing else but socialism. The converse theorem: the monstrous growth of state coercion in the USSR is eloquent testimony that society is moving away from socialism.

12. "The working men have no country." These words of the Manifesto have more than once been evaluated by philistines as an agitational quip. As a matter of fact they provided the proletariat with the sole conceivable directive in the question of the capitalist "fatherland." The violation of this directive by the Second International brought about not only four years of devastation in Europe,[5] but the present stagnation of world culture. In view of the impending new war, for which the betrayal of the Third International has paved the way, the Manifesto remains even now the most reliable counselor on the question of the capitalist "fatherland."

Thus, we see that the joint and rather brief production of two young authors still continues to give irreplaceable directives upon the most important and burning questions of the struggle for emancipation. What other book could even distantly be compared with the *Communist Manifesto*? But this does not imply that, after ninety years of unprecedented development of productive forces and vast social struggles, the Manifesto needs neither corrections nor additions. Revolutionary thought has nothing in common with idol-worship. Programs and prognoses are tested and corrected in the light of experience, which is the supreme criterion of human reason. The Manifesto, too, requires corrections and additions. However, as is evidenced by historical experience itself, these corrections and additions can be successfully made only by proceeding in accord with the method lodged in the foundation of the Manifesto itself. We shall try to indicate this in several most important instances.

1. Marx taught that no social system departs from the arena of history before exhausting its creative potentialities. The Manifesto excoriates capitalism for retarding the development of the productive forces. During that period, however, as well as in the following decades, this retardation was only relative in nature. Had it been possible in the second half of the nineteenth century to organize economy on socialist beginnings, its tempos of growth would have been immeasurably greater. But this theoretically irrefutable postulate does not, however, invalidate the fact that the productive forces kept expanding on a world scale right up to the world war. Only in the last twenty years, despite the most modern conquests of science and technology, has the epoch begun of out-and-out stagnation and even decline of world economy. Mankind is beginning to expend its accumulated capital, while the next war threatens to destroy the very foundations of civilization for many years to come. The authors of the Manifesto thought that capitalism would be scrapped long prior to the time when, from a relatively reactionary regime, it would turn into an absolutely reactionary regime. This transformation took final shape only before the eyes of the present generation, and changed our epoch into the epoch of

wars, revolutions, and fascism.

2. The error of Marx and Engels in regard to the historical dates flowed, on the one hand, from an underestimation of future possibilities latent in capitalism and, on the other, from an overestimation of the revolutionary maturity of the proletariat. The revolution of 1848 did not turn into a socialist revolution as the Manifesto had calculated but opened up to Germany the possibility of a vast future capitalist ascension. The Paris Commune proved that the proletariat, without having a tempered revolutionary party at its head, cannot wrest power from the bourgeoisie.[6] Meanwhile, the prolonged period of capitalist prosperity that ensued brought about not the education of the revolutionary vanguard, but rather the bourgeois degeneration of the labor aristocracy, which became in turn the chief brake on the proletarian revolution. In the nature of things, the authors of the Manifesto could not possibly have foreseen this "dialectic."

3. For the Manifesto, capitalism was—the kingdom of free competition. While referring to the growing concentration of capital, the Manifesto did not draw the necessary conclusion in regard to monopoly, which has become the dominant capitalist form in our epoch and the most important precondition for socialist economy. Only afterwards, in *Capital,* did Marx establish the tendency toward the transformation of free competition into monopoly. It was Lenin who gave a scientific characterization of monopoly capitalism in his *Imperialism.*

4. Basing themselves primarily on the example of "industrial revolution" in England, the authors of the Manifesto pictured far too unilaterally the process of liquidation of the intermediate classes, as a wholesale proletarianization

of crafts, petty trades, and peasantry. In point of fact, the elemental forces of competition have far from completed this simultaneously progressive and barbarous work. Capitalism has ruined the petty bourgeoisie at a much faster rate than it has proletarianized it. Furthermore, the bourgeois state has long directed its conscious policy toward the artificial maintenance of petty-bourgeois strata. At the opposite pole, the growth of technology and the rationalization of large-scale industry engenders chronic unemployment and obstructs the proletarianization of the petty bourgeoisie. Concurrently, the development of capitalism has accelerated in the extreme the growth of legions of technicians, administrators, commercial employees, in short, the so-called new middle class. In consequence, the intermediate classes, to whose disappearance the Manifesto so categorically refers, comprise even in a country as highly industrialized as Germany, about one-half of the population. However, the artificial preservation of antiquated petty-bourgeois strata nowise mitigates the social contradictions, but, on the contrary, invests them with an especial malignancy, and together with the permanent army of the unemployed constitutes the most malevolent expression of the *decay* of capitalism.

5. Calculated for a revolutionary epoch, the Manifesto contains (end of chapter II) ten demands, corresponding to the period of direct transition from capitalism to socialism. In their preface of 1872, Marx and Engels declared these demands to be in part antiquated, and, in any case, only of secondary importance. The reformists seized upon this evaluation to interpret it in the sense that transitional revolutionary demands had forever ceded their place to the social democratic "minimum program," which, as is well

known, does not transcend the limits of bourgeois democracy. As a matter of fact, the authors of the Manifesto indicated quite precisely the main correction of their transitional program, namely, "the working class cannot simply lay hold of the ready-made state machinery, and wield it for its own purposes." In other words, the correction was directed against the fetishism of bourgeois democracy. Marx later counterposed to the capitalist state, the state of the type of the Commune. This "type" subsequently assumed the much more graphic shape of soviets. There cannot be a revolutionary program today without *soviets* and without *workers control*. As for the rest, the ten demands of the Manifesto, which appeared "archaic" in an epoch of peaceful parliamentary activity, have today regained completely their true significance. The social democratic "minimum program," on the other hand, has become hopelessly antiquated.

6. Basing its expectation that "the bourgeois revolution in Germany will be but the prelude to an immediately following proletarian revolution," the Manifesto cites the much more advanced conditions of European civilization as compared with what existed in England in the seventeenth century and in France in the eighteenth century, and the far greater development of the proletariat. The error in this prognosis was not only in the date. The revolution of 1848 revealed within a few months that precisely under more advanced conditions, none of the bourgeois classes is capable of bringing the revolution to its termination: the big and middle bourgeoisie is far too closely linked with the landowners and fettered by the fear of the masses; the petty bourgeoisie is far too divided and, in its leading tops, far too dependent on the big bourgeoisie. As

evidenced by the entire subsequent course of development in Europe and Asia, the bourgeois revolution, taken by itself, can no more in general be consummated. A complete purge of feudal rubbish from society is conceivable only on the condition that the proletariat, freed from the influence of bourgeois parties, can take its stand at the head of the peasantry and establish its revolutionary dictatorship. By this token, the bourgeois revolution becomes interlaced with the first stage of the socialist revolution, subsequently to dissolve in the latter. The national revolution therewith becomes a link of the world revolution. The transformation of the economic foundation and of all social relations assumes a permanent (uninterrupted) character.

For revolutionary parties in backward countries of Asia, Latin America, and Africa, a clear understanding of the organic connection between the democratic revolution and the dictatorship of the proletariat—and thereby, the international socialist revolution—is a life-and-death question.

7. While depicting how capitalism draws into its vortex backward and barbarous countries, the Manifesto contains no reference to the struggle of colonial and semicolonial countries for independence. To the extent that Marx and Engels considered the social revolution "in the leading civilized countries at least," to be a matter of the next few years, the colonial question was resolved automatically for them, not in consequence of an independent movement of oppressed nationalities but in consequence of the victory of the proletariat in the metropolitan centers of capitalism. The questions of revolutionary strategy in colonial and semicolonial countries are therefore not touched upon at all by the Manifesto. Yet these questions demand an independent solution. For example, it is quite self-evident that while the

"national fatherland" has become the most baneful historical brake in advanced capitalist countries, it still remains
a relatively progressive factor in backward countries compelled to struggle for an independent existence.

"The Communists," declares the Manifesto, "everywhere
support every revolutionary movement against the existing
social and political order of things." The movement of the
colored races against their imperialist oppressors is one of
the most important and powerful movements against the
existing order and therefore calls for the complete, uncon-
ditional, and unlimited support on the part of the proletariat of the white race. The credit for developing revolutionary strategy for oppressed nationalities belongs primarily
to Lenin.

8. The most antiquated section of the Manifesto—not
with respect to method but material—is the criticism of "socialist" literature for the first part of the nineteenth century
(chapter III) and the definition of the position of the Communists in relation to various opposition parties (chapter IV).
The movements and parties listed in the Manifesto were so
drastically swept away either by the revolution of 1848 or
the ensuing counterrevolution that one must look up even
their names in a historical dictionary. However, in this section, too, the Manifesto is perhaps closer to us now than it
was to the previous generation. In the epoch of the flow-
ering of the Second International when Marxism seemed
to exert an undivided sway, the ideas of pre-Marxist socialism could have been considered as having receded decisively into the past. Things are otherwise today. The de-
composition of the social democracy and the Communist
International at every step engenders monstrous ideological relapses. Senile thought seems to have become infan-

tile. In search of all-saving formulas, the prophets in the epoch of decline discover anew doctrines long since buried by scientific socialism.

As touches the question of opposition parties, it is in this domain that the elapsed decades have introduced the most deep-going changes, not only in the sense that the old parties have long been brushed aside by new ones, but also in the sense that the very character of parties and their mutual relations have radically changed in the conditions of the imperialist epoch. The Manifesto must therefore be amplified with the most important documents of the first four congresses of the Communist International, the essential literature of Bolshevism, and the decisions of the conferences of the Fourth International.[7]

We have already remarked above that according to Marx, no social order departs from the scene without first exhausting the potentialities latent in it. However, even an antiquated social order does not cede its place to a new order without resistance. A change in social regimes presupposes the harshest form of the class struggle, i.e., revolution. If the proletariat, for one reason or another, proves incapable of overthrowing with an audacious blow the outlived bourgeois order, then finance capital in the struggle to maintain its unstable rule can do nothing but turn the petty bourgeoisie, ruined and demoralized by it, into the pogrom army of fascism. The bourgeois degeneration of the social democracy and the fascist degeneration of the petty bourgeoisie are interlinked as cause and effect.

At the present time, the Third International, far more wantonly than the Second, performs in all countries the work of deceiving and demoralizing the toilers. By massacring the vanguard of the Spanish proletariat, the unbridled hirelings of Moscow not only pave the way for fascism but execute a goodly share of its labors. The protracted crisis of the international revolution, which is turning more and more into a crisis of human culture, is reducible in its essentials to the crisis of revolutionary leadership.

As the heir to the great tradition, of which the *Manifesto of the Communist Party* forms the most precious link, the Fourth International is educating new cadres for the solution of old tasks. Theory is generalized reality. In an honest attitude to revolutionary theory is expressed the impassioned urge to reconstruct the social reality. That in the southern part of the "Dark Continent" our co-thinkers were the first to translate the Manifesto into the Afrikaans language is another graphic illustration of the fact that Marxist thought lives today only under the banner of the Fourth International. To it belongs the future. When the centennial of the *Communist Manifesto* is celebrated, the Fourth International will have become the decisive revolutionary force on our planet.

Preface to the German edition of 1872

BY KARL MARX AND FREDERICK ENGELS

THE COMMUNIST LEAGUE,[8] an international association of workers, which could of course be only a secret one under the conditions obtaining at the time, commissioned the undersigned, at the congress held in London in November 1847, to draw up for publication a detailed theoretical and practical program of the party. Such was the origin of the following Manifesto, the manuscript of which traveled to London, to be printed, a few weeks before the February revolution.[9] First published in German, it has been republished in that language in at least twelve different editions in Germany, England, and America. It was published in English for the first time in 1850 in the *Red Republican*,[10] London, translated by Miss Helen Macfarlane, and in 1871 in at least three different translations in America. A French version first appeared in Paris shortly before the June insurrection of 1848[11] and recently in *Le Socialiste*[12] of New York. A new translation is in the course of preparation. A Polish version appeared in London shortly after it was first published in German. A Russian translation was published in Geneva in the sixties. Into Danish, too, it was translated shortly after its first appearance.

Written by Marx and Engels for the German edition published in Leipzig, Germany, in 1872.

However much the state of things may have altered during the last twenty-five years, the general principles laid down in this Manifesto are, on the whole, as correct today as ever. Here and there some detail might be improved. The practical application of the principles will depend, as the Manifesto itself states, everywhere and at all times on the historical conditions for the time being existing, and, for that reason, no special stress is laid on the revolutionary measures proposed at the end of section II. That passage would, in many respects, be very differently worded today. In view of the gigantic strides of modern industry in the last twenty-five years, and of the accompanying improved and extended party organization of the working class, in view of the practical experience gained, first in the February revolution, and then, still more, in the Paris Commune, where the proletariat for the first time held political power for two whole months, this program has in some details become antiquated. One thing especially was proved by the Commune, namely, that "the working class cannot simply lay hold of the ready-made State machinery, and wield it for its own purposes." (See *The Civil War in France: Address of the General Council of the International Working Men's Association*, London, Truelove, 1871, p. 15, where this point is further developed.[13]) Further, it is self-evident that the criticism of socialist literature is deficient in relation to the present time, because it comes down only to 1847; also, that the remarks on the relation of the communists to the various opposition parties (section IV), although in principle still correct, yet in practice are antiquated, because the political situation has been entirely changed, and the progress of history has swept from off the earth the greater portion of the political parties there enumerated.

But, then, the Manifesto has become a historical document which we have no longer any right to alter. A subsequent edition may perhaps appear with an introduction bridging the gap from 1847 to the present day; this reprint was too unexpected to leave us time for that.

Karl Marx, Frederick Engels
LONDON, JUNE 24, 1872

From the preface
to the German edition of 1890

BY FREDERICK ENGELS

THE MANIFESTO has had a history of its own. Greeted with enthusiasm at the time of its appearance, by the then still not at all numerous vanguard of scientific socialism (as is proved by the translations mentioned in the first preface), it was soon forced into the background by the reaction that began with the defeat of the Paris workers in June 1848 and was finally excommunicated "according to law" by the conviction of the Cologne Communists in November 1852.[14] With the disappearance from the public scene of the workers movement that had begun with the February revolution, the Manifesto too passed into the background.

When the working class of Europe had again gathered sufficient strength for a new onslaught upon the power of the ruling classes, the International Working Men's Association came into being. Its aim was to weld together into *one* huge army the whole militant working class of Europe and America. Therefore it could not *set out* from the principles laid down in the Manifesto. It was bound to have a program which would not shut the door on the English trade unions; the French, Belgian, Italian, and Spanish

Written by Engels for the German edition which appeared in London in 1890.

25

Proudhonists; and the German Lassalleans.* This program—the preamble to the rules of the International[15]—was drawn up by Marx with a master hand acknowledged even by Bakunin and the anarchists. For the ultimate triumph of the ideas set forth in the Manifesto, Marx relied solely and exclusively upon the intellectual development of the working class, as it necessarily had to ensue from united action and discussion. The events and vicissitudes in the struggle against capital, the defeats even more than the successes, could not but demonstrate to the fighters the inadequacy hitherto of their universal panaceas and make their minds more receptive to a thorough understanding of the true conditions for the emancipation of the workers. And Marx was right. The working class of 1874, at the dissolution of the International, was altogether different from that of 1864, at its foundation. Proudhonism in the Latin countries and the specific Lassalleanism in Germany were dying out, and even the then arch-conservative English trade unions were gradually approaching the point where in 1887 the chairman of their Swansea congress could say in their name: "Continental socialism has lost its terrors for us." Yet by 1887 Continental socialism was almost exclusively the theory heralded in the Manifesto. Thus, to a certain extent, the history of the Manifesto reflects the history of the modern working-class movement since 1848. At pres-

---

* Lassalle personally, to us, always acknowledged himself to be a "disciple" of Marx, and, as such, stood, of course, on the ground of the Manifesto. Matters were quite different with regard to those of his followers who did not go beyond his demand for producers' cooperatives supported by state credits and who divided the whole working class into supporters of state assistance and supporters of self-assistance. [*Note by Engels.*]

ent it is doubtless the most widely circulated, the most international product of all socialist literature, the common program of many millions of workers of all countries, from Siberia to California.

Nevertheless, when it appeared we could not have called it a *Socialist* Manifesto. In 1847 two kinds of people were considered socialists. On the one hand were the adherents of the various utopian systems, notably the Owenites in England and the Fourierists in France, both of whom at that date had already dwindled to mere sects gradually dying out. On the other, the manifold types of social quacks who wanted to eliminate social abuses through their various universal panaceas and all kinds of patchwork, without hurting capital and profit in the least. In both cases, people who stood outside the labor movement and who looked for support rather to the "educated" classes. The section of the working class, however, which demanded a radical reconstruction of society, convinced that mere political revolutions were not enough, then called itself *communist.* It was still a rough-hewn, only instinctive, and frequently somewhat crude communism. Yet it was powerful enough to bring into being two systems of utopian communism—in France the "Icarian" communism of Cabet and in Germany that of Weitling. Socialism in 1847 signified a bourgeois movement, communism a working-class movement. Socialism was, on the Continent at least, quite respectable, whereas communism was the very opposite. And since we were very decidedly of the opinion as early as then that "the emancipation of the workers must be the act of the working class itself," we could have no hesitations as to which of the two names we should choose. Nor has it ever occurred to us since to repudiate it.

✦ "Working men of all countries, unite!" But few voices responded when we proclaimed these words to the world forty-two years ago, on the eve of the first Paris revolution in which the proletariat came out with demands of its own.[16] On September 28, 1864, however, the proletarians of most of the western European countries united to form the International Working Men's Association of glorious memory. True, the International itself lived only nine years. But that the eternal union of the proletarians of all countries created by it is still alive and lives stronger than ever, there is no better witness than this day. Because today,[17] as I write these lines, the European and American proletariat is reviewing its fighting forces, mobilized for the first time, mobilized as *one* army, under *one* flag, for *one* immediate aim: the standard eight-hour working day, to be established by legal enactment, as proclaimed by the Geneva congress of the International in 1866 and again by the Paris workers' congress in 1889. And today's spectacle will open the eyes of the capitalists and landlords of all countries to the fact that today the working men of all countries are united indeed.

If only Marx were still by my side to see this with his own eyes!

Frederick Engels
LONDON, MAY I, 1890

[Handwritten annotations:] nobality, pass down their title to their inheritance. middle age → 1400 → trading people become wealthy. befor 1789 - Europe - controled by kings and upper class. rulling class + rich bussiness owner.

Manifesto of
the Communist Party

[Handwritten:] they power in old system

[Handwritten:] French 1789 revolution: Middle poor people revolt and take power from the upper class.

BY KARL MARX AND FREDERICK ENGELS

[Handwritten:] 1799 = strongest man in military. they should have right. he crowned himself emperor. he wasnt a rulling class before

A SPECTRE IS HAUNTING EUROPE—the spectre of communism. All the powers of old Europe have entered into a holy alliance to exorcise this spectre: pope and czar, Metternich and Guizot,[18] French Radicals and German police spies.

Where is the party in opposition that has not been decried as communistic by its opponents in power? Where the opposition that has not hurled back the branding reproach of communism, against the more advanced opposition parties, as well as against its reactionary adversaries?

[Handwritten:] ghost ... communism ... he charged as the revolt

Two things result from this fact.

I. Communism is already acknowledged by all European powers to be itself a power.

II. It is high time that communists should openly, in the face of the whole world, publish their views, their aims, their tendencies, and meet this nursery tale of the spectre of communism with a manifesto of the party itself.

[Handwritten:] need to get together to write down what they believe in. So the other people can't say the false thing. slander

[Handwritten left margin:] 1814 the battle of waterloo

Written in December 1847–January 1848; published originally in German in London in February 1848. It is printed here according to the English-language translation of 1888 edited by Frederick Engels. It also includes footnotes by Engels added to the 1890 German edition.

[Handwritten bottom:] 1815 congress of Viena. Attempted to put back the traditional rullers

To this end, communists of various nationalities have assembled in London, and sketched the following Manifesto, to be published in the English, French, German, Italian, Flemish, and Danish languages.

Middle class

I. Bourgeois and proletarians*

poor people labor

The history of all hitherto existing society† is the history of class struggles.

Freeman and slave, patrician and plebeian, lord and serf, *rural slave* guildmaster‡ and journeyman, in a word, oppressor and oppressed, stood in constant opposition to one another, car-

---

* By bourgeoisie is meant the class of modern capitalists, owners of the means of social production and employers of wage labor. By proletariat, the class of modern wage-laborers who, having no means of production of their own, are reduced to selling their labor power in order to live. [*Note by Engels to the English edition of 1888.*]

† That is, all *written* history. In 1847, the prehistory of society, the social organization existing previous to recorded history, was all but unknown. Since then, Haxthausen discovered common ownership of land in Russia, Maurer proved it to be the social foundation from which all Teutonic races started in history, and by and by village communities were found to be, or to have been, the primitive form of society everywhere from India to Ireland. The inner organization of this primitive communistic society was laid bare, in its typical form, by Morgan's crowning discovery of the true nature of the *gens* and its relation to the *tribe*. With the dissolution of these primeval communities, society begins to be differentiated into separate and finally antagonistic classes. I have attempted to retrace this process of dissolution in *The Origin of the Family, Private Property and the State.* [*Note by Engels to the English edition of 1888.*]

‡ Guildmaster, that is, a full member of a guild, a master within, not a head of a guild. [*Note by Engels to the English edition of 1888.*]

Dialectic

ried on an uninterrupted, now hidden, now open fight, a fight that each time ended either in a revolutionary reconstitution of society at large or in the common ruin of the contending classes.

In the earlier epochs of history, we find almost everywhere a complicated arrangement of society into various orders, a manifold gradation of social rank. In ancient Rome we have patricians, knights, plebeians, slaves; in the Middle Ages, feudal lords, vassals, guildmasters, journeymen, apprentices, serfs; in almost all of these classes, again, subordinate gradations.

The modern bourgeois society that has sprouted from the ruins of feudal society has not done away with class antagonisms. It has but established new classes, new conditions of oppression, new forms of struggle in place of the old ones.

Our epoch, the epoch of the bourgeoisie, possesses, however, this distinctive feature: it has simplified the class antagonisms. Society as a whole is more and more splitting up into two great hostile camps, into two great classes directly facing each other: bourgeoisie and proletariat.

From the serfs of the Middle Ages sprang the chartered burghers of the earliest towns. From these burgesses the first elements of the bourgeoisie were developed.

The discovery of America, the rounding of the Cape, opened up fresh ground for the rising bourgeoisie. The East Indian and Chinese markets, the colonization of America, trade with the colonies, the increase in the means of exchange and in commodities generally, gave to commerce, to navigation, to industry, an impulse never before known, and thereby, to the revolutionary element in the tottering feudal society, a rapid development.

Market oppened up.

The feudal system of industry, under which industrial production was monopolized by closed guilds, now no longer sufficed for the growing wants of the new markets. *Many workshop* The manufacturing system took its place. The guildmasters were pushed on one side by the manufacturing middle class; division of labor between the different corporate guilds vanished in the face of division of labor in each single workshop.

Labor want enough machine Meantime the markets kept ever growing, the demand ever rising. Even manufacture no longer sufficed. Thereupon, steam and machinery revolutionized industrial production. The place of manufacture was taken by the giant, modern industry, the place of the industrial middle class, by industrial millionaires, the leaders of whole industrial armies, the modern bourgeois.

Modern industry has established the world market, for which the discovery of America paved the way. This market has given an immense development to commerce, to navigation, to communication by land. This development has, in its turn, reacted on the extension of industry; and in proportion as industry, commerce, navigation, railways extended, in the same proportion the bourgeoisie developed, increased its capital, and pushed into the background every class handed down from the Middle Ages.

We see, therefore, how the modern bourgeoisie is itself the product of a long course of development, of a series of revolutions in the modes of production and of exchange. *new global industrial trade*

Each step in the development of the bourgeoisie was accompanied by a corresponding political advance of that class. An oppressed class under the sway of the feudal nobility, an armed and self-governing association in the me-

dieval commune;* here independent urban republic (as in
Italy and Germany), there taxable "third estate" of the monarchy (as in France), afterwards, in the period of manufacture proper, serving either the semifeudal or the absolute
monarchy as a counterpoise against the nobility, and, in
fact, cornerstone of the great monarchies in general, the
bourgeoisie has at last, since the establishment of modern
industry and of the world market, conquered for itself, in
the modern representative state, exclusive political sway.
The executive of the modern state is but a committee for
managing the common affairs of the whole bourgeoisie.

The bourgeoisie, historically, has played a most revolutionary part.

The bourgeoisie, wherever it has gotten the upper hand,
has put an end to all feudal, patriarchal, idyllic relations. It
has pitilessly torn asunder the motley feudal ties that bound
man to his "natural superiors," and has left remaining no
other nexus between man and man than naked self-interest,
than callous "cash payment." It has drowned the most heav-
enly ecstasies of religious fervor, of chivalrous enthusiasm,
of philistine sentimentalism, in the icy water of egotistical
calculation. It has resolved personal worth into exchange
value, and in place of the numberless indefeasible chartered

---

* "Commune" was the name taken, in France, by the nascent towns
even before they had conquered from their feudal lords and masters
local self-government and political rights as the "Third Estate." Generally speaking, for the economic development of the bourgeoisie, England is here taken as the typical country; for its political development,
France. [*Note by Engels to the English edition of 1888.*]

This was the name given their urban communities by the townsmen
of Italy and France, after they had purchased or wrested their initial
rights of self-government from their feudal lords. [*Note by Engels to
the German edition of 1890.*]

bourgeesie has take away the spirit

freedoms, has set up that single, unconscionable freedom—free trade. In one word, for exploitation, veiled by religious and political illusions, it has substituted naked, shameless, direct, brutal exploitation.

The bourgeoisie has stripped of its halo every occupation hitherto honored and looked up to with reverent awe. It has converted the physician, the lawyer, the priest, the poet, the man of science, into its paid wage-laborers.

The bourgeoisie has torn away from the family its sentimental veil and has reduced the family relation to a mere money relation.

The bourgeoisie has disclosed how it came to pass that the brutal display of vigor in the Middle Ages, which Reactionists so much admire, found its fitting complement in the most slothful indolence. It has been the first to show what man's activity can bring about. It has accomplished wonders far surpassing Egyptian pyramids, Roman aqueducts, and Gothic cathedrals; it has conducted expeditions that put in the shade all former exoduses of nations and crusades.[19]

The bourgeoisie cannot exist without constantly revolutionizing the instruments of production, and thereby the relations of production, and with them the whole relations of society. Conservation of the old modes of production in unaltered form was, on the contrary, the first condition of existence for all earlier industrial classes. Constant revolutionizing of production, uninterrupted disturbance of all social conditions, everlasting uncertainty and agitation distinguish the bourgeois epoch from all earlier ones. All fixed, fast-frozen relations, with their train of ancient and venerable prejudices and opinions, are swept away, all new-formed ones become antiquated before they can ossify.

sarcastic

ho value in art

in anything else unless money

competition

Darwin?

in competition with everyone else.

you can't escape

All that is solid melts into air, all that is holy is profaned, and man is at last compelled to face, with sober senses, his real conditions of life and his relations with his kind.

The need of a constantly expanding market for its products chases the bourgeoisie over the whole surface of the globe. It must nestle everywhere, settle everywhere, establish connections everywhere.

The bourgeoisie has, through its exploitation of the world market, given a cosmopolitan character to production and consumption in every country. To the great chagrin of Reactionists, it has drawn from under the feet of industry the national ground on which it stood. All old-established national industries have been destroyed or are daily being destroyed. They are dislodged by new industries, whose introduction becomes a life-and-death question for all civilized nations, by industries that no longer work up indigenous raw material, but raw material drawn from the remotest zones; industries whose products are consumed not only at home, but in every quarter of the globe. In place of the old wants, satisfied by the productions of the country, we find new wants, requiring for their satisfaction the products of distant lands and climes. In place of the old local and national seclusion and self-sufficiency, we have intercourse in every direction, universal interdependence of nations. And as in material, so also in intellectual production. The intellectual creations of individual nations become common property. National one-sidedness and narrow-mindedness become more and more impossible, and from the numerous national and local literatures, there arises a world literature.

The bourgeoisie, by the rapid improvement of all instruments of production, by the immensely facilitated means of communication, draws all, even the most barbarian, nations into civilization. The cheap prices of its commodities are the heavy artillery with which it batters down all Chinese walls, with which it forces the barbarians' intensely obstinate hatred of foreigners to capitulate. It compels all nations, on pain of extinction, to adopt the bourgeois mode of production; it compels them to introduce what it calls civilization into their midst, i.e., to become bourgeois themselves. In one word, it creates a world after its own image.

The bourgeoisie has subjected the country to the rule of the towns. It has created enormous cities, has greatly increased the urban population as compared with the rural, and has thus rescued a considerable part of the population from the idiocy of rural life. Just as it has made the country dependent on the towns, so it has made barbarian and semibarbarian countries dependent on the civilized ones, nations of peasants on nations of bourgeois, the East on the West.

The bourgeoisie keeps more and more doing away with the scattered state of the population, of the means of production, and of property. It has agglomerated population, centralized means of production, and has concentrated property in a few hands. The necessary consequence of this was political centralization. Independent, or but loosely connected provinces, with separate interests, laws, governments, and systems of taxation, became lumped together into one nation, with one government, one code of laws, one national class interest, one frontier, and one customs tariff.

The bourgeoisie, during its rule of scarce one hundred years, has created more massive and more colossal productive forces than have all preceding generations together. Subjection of nature's forces to man, machinery, application of chemistry to industry and agriculture, steam navigation, railways, electric telegraphs, clearing of whole continents for cultivation, canalization of rivers, whole populations conjured out of the ground—what earlier century had even a presentiment that such productive forces slumbered in the lap of social labor?

We see then: the means of production and of exchange, on whose foundation the bourgeoisie built itself up, were generated in feudal society. At a certain stage in the development of these means of production and of exchange, the conditions under which feudal society produced and exchanged, the feudal organization of agriculture and manufacturing industry, in one word, the feudal relations of property, became no longer compatible with the already developed productive forces; they became so many fetters. They had to be burst asunder; they were burst asunder.

Into their place stepped free competition, accompanied by a social and political constitution adapted to it and by the economic and political sway of the bourgeois class.

A similar movement is going on before our own eyes. Modern bourgeois society with its relations of production, of exchange, and of property, a society that has conjured up such gigantic means of production and of exchange, is like the sorcerer who is no longer able to control the powers of the nether world whom he has called up by his spells. For many a decade past, the history of industry and commerce is but the history of the revolt of modern productive forces against modern conditions of production, against the property relations that are the conditions for the existence of the bourgeoisie and of its rule. It is enough to mention the commercial crises that by their periodic return put on trial, each time more threateningly, the existence of the entire bourgeois society. In these crises a great part not only of the existing products, but also of the previously created productive forces are periodically destroyed. In these crises there breaks out an epidemic that, in all earlier epochs, would have seemed an absurdity—the epidemic of over-production. Society suddenly finds itself put back into a state of momentary barbarism; it appears as if a famine, a universal war of devastation, had cut off the supply of every means of subsistence; industry and commerce seem to be destroyed; and why? Because there is too much civilization, too much means of subsistence, too much industry, too much commerce. The productive forces at the disposal of society no longer tend to further the development of the conditions of bourgeois property; on the contrary, they have become too powerful for these conditions, by which they are fettered, and so soon as they overcome these fetters, they bring disorder into the whole of bourgeois society, endanger the existence of bourgeois property. The conditions of bourgeois society are too narrow to comprise the wealth created by them. And how does the bourgeoisie get over these crises? On the one hand by enforced destruction of a mass of productive forces; on the other, by the conquest of new markets and by the more thorough exploitation of the old ones. That is to say, by paving the way for more extensive and more destructive crises and by diminishing the means whereby crises are prevented.

The weapons with which the bourgeoisie felled feudalism to the ground are now turned against the bourgeoisie itself.

But not only has the bourgeoisie forged the weapons that bring death to itself; it has also called into existence the men who are to wield those weapons—the modern working class—the proletarians.

In proportion as the bourgeoisie, i.e., capital, is developed, in the same proportion is the proletariat, the modern working class, developed—a class of laborers, who live only so long as they find work and who find work only so long as their labor increases capital. These laborers, who must sell themselves piecemeal, are a commodity, like every other article of commerce, and are consequently exposed to all the vicissitudes of competition, to all the fluctuations of the market.

Owing to the extensive use of machinery, and to division of labor, the work of the proletarians has lost all individual character and, consequently, all charm for the workman. He becomes an appendage of the machine, and it is only the most simple, most monotonous, and most easily acquired knack that is required of him. Hence, the cost of production of a workman is restricted, almost entirely, to the means of subsistence that he requires for his maintenance and for the propagation of his race. But the price of a commodity, and therefore also of labor,[20] is equal to its cost of production. In proportion, therefore, as the repulsiveness of the work increases, the wage decreases. Nay more, in proportion as the use of machinery and division of labor increases, in the same proportion the burden of toil also increases, whether by prolongation of the working hours, by increase of the work exacted in a given time, or by increased speed of machinery, etc.

Modern industry has converted the little workshop of the patriarchal master into the great factory of the industrial capitalist. Masses of laborers, crowded into the factory, are organized like soldiers. As privates of the industrial army they are placed under the command of a perfect hierarchy of officers and sergeants. Not only are they slaves of the bourgeois class and of the bourgeois state; they are daily and hourly enslaved by the machine, by the overlooker, and, above all, by the individual bourgeois manufacturer himself. The more openly this despotism proclaims gain to be its end and aim, the more petty, the more hateful, and the more embittering it is.

The less the skill and exertion of strength implied in manual labor, in other words, the more modern industry becomes developed, the more is the labor of men superseded by that of women. Differences of age and sex have no longer any distinctive social validity for the working class. All are instruments of labor, more or less expensive to use, according to their age and sex.

No sooner is the exploitation of the laborer by the manufacturer, so far, at an end, and he receives his wages in cash, than he is set upon by the other portions of the bourgeoisie, the landlord, the shopkeeper, the pawnbroker, etc.

The lower strata of the middle class—the small trades people, shopkeepers, and retired tradesmen generally, the handicraftsmen and peasants—all these sink gradually into the proletariat, partly because their diminutive capital does not suffice for the scale on which modern industry is carried on and is swamped in the competition with the large capitalists, partly because their specialized skill is rendered worthless by new methods of production. Thus the proletariat is recruited from all classes of the population.

The proletariat goes through various stages of development. With its birth begins its struggle with the bourgeoisie. At first the contest is carried on by individual laborers, then by the work people of a factory, then by the operatives of one trade, in one locality, against the individual bourgeois who directly exploits them. They direct their attacks not against the bourgeois conditions of production, but against the instruments of production themselves; they destroy imported wares that compete with their labor, they smash to pieces machinery, they set factories ablaze, they seek to restore by force the vanished status of the workman of the Middle Ages.

At this stage the laborers still form an incoherent mass scattered over the whole country and broken up by their mutual competition. If anywhere they unite to form more compact bodies, this is not yet the consequence of their own active union but of the union of the bourgeoisie, which class, in order to attain its own political ends, is compelled to set the whole proletariat in motion and is moreover yet, for a time, able to do so. At this stage, therefore, the proletarians do not fight their enemies, but the enemies of their enemies, the remnants of absolute monarchy, the landowners, the nonindustrial bourgeois, the petty bourgeoisie. Thus the whole historical movement is concentrated in the hands of the bourgeoisie; every victory so obtained is a victory for the bourgeoisie.

But with the development of industry the proletariat not only increases in number; it becomes concentrated in greater masses, its strength grows, and it feels that strength more. The various interests and conditions of life within the ranks of the proletariat are more and more equalized, in proportion as machinery obliterates all distinctions of labor and nearly everywhere reduces wages to the same low level. The growing competition among the bourgeois, and the resulting commercial crises, make the wages of the workers ever more fluctuating. The unceasing improvement of machinery, ever more rapidly developing, makes their livelihood more and more precarious; the collisions between individual workmen and individual bourgeois take more and more the character of collisions between two classes. Thereupon the workers begin to form combinations (trades unions) against the bourgeois; they club together in order to keep up the rate of wages; they found permanent associations in order to make provision beforehand for these occasional revolts. Here and there the contest breaks out into riots.

Now and then the workers are victorious, but only for a time. The real fruit of their battles lies, not in the immediate result, but in the ever-expanding union of the workers. This union is helped on by the improved means of communication that are created by modern industry and that place the workers of different localities in contact with one another. It was just this contact that was needed to centralize the numerous local struggles, all of the same character, into one national struggle between classes. But every class struggle is a political struggle. And that union, to attain which the burghers of the Middle Ages, with their miserable highways, required centuries, the modern proletarians, thanks to railways, achieve in a few years.

This organization of the proletarians into a class, and consequently into a political party, is continually being upset again by the competition between the workers themselves. But it ever rises up again, stronger, firmer, mightier. It compels legislative recognition of particular interests of the workers, by taking advantage of the divisions among the bourgeoisie itself. Thus the ten-hours bill in England was carried.

Altogether collisions between the classes of the old society further, in many ways, the course of development of the proletariat. The bourgeoisie finds itself involved in a constant battle. At first with the aristocracy; later on, with those portions of the bourgeoisie itself whose interests have become antagonistic to the progress of industry; at all times, with the bourgeoisie of foreign countries. In all these battles it sees itself compelled to appeal to the proletariat, to ask for its help, and thus to drag it into the political arena. The bourgeoisie itself, therefore, supplies the proletariat with its own elements of political and general education; in other words, it furnishes the proletariat with weapons for fighting the bourgeoisie.

Further, as we have already seen, entire sections of the ruling classes are, by the advance of industry, precipitated into the proletariat or are at least threatened in their conditions of existence. These also supply the proletariat with fresh elements of enlightenment and progress.

Finally, in times when the class struggle nears the decisive hour, the process of dissolution going on within the ruling class, in fact within the whole range of old society, assumes such a violent, glaring character, that a small section of the ruling class cuts itself adrift, and joins the revolutionary class, the class that holds the future in its hands. Just as, therefore, at an earlier period a section of the nobility went over to the bourgeoisie, so now a portion of the bourgeoisie goes over to the proletariat, and in particular, a portion of the bourgeois ideologists who have raised themselves to the level of comprehending theoretically the historical movement as a whole.

Of all the classes that stand face to face with the bourgeoisie today, the proletariat alone is a really revolutionary class. The other classes decay and finally disapp␣␣␣ in the face of modern industry; the proletariat is its ␣

and essential product.

The lower middle class, the small manufacturer, the shopkeeper, the artisan, the peasant, all these fight against the bourgeoisie to save from extinction their existence as fractions of the middle class. They are therefore not revolutionary, but conservative. Nay more, they are reactionary, for they try to roll back the wheel of history. If by chance they are revolutionary, they are so only in view of their impending transfer into the proletariat, they thus defend not their present, but their future interests, they desert their own standpoint to place themselves at that of the proletariat.

The "dangerous class," the social scum, that passively rotting mass thrown off by the lowest layers of the old society, may, here and there, be swept into the movement by a proletarian revolution; its conditions of life, however, prepare it far more for the part of a bribed tool of reactionary intrigue.

In the conditions of the proletariat, those of old society at large are already virtually swamped. The proletarian is without property; his relation to his wife and children has no longer anything in common with the bourgeois family relations; modern industrial labor, modern subjection to capital, the same in England as in France, in America as in Germany, has stripped him of every trace of national character. Law, morality, religion are to him so many bourgeois prejudices, behind which lurk in ambush just as many bourgeois interests.

All the preceding classes that got the upper hand sought to fortify their already acquired status by subjecting society at large to their conditions of appropriation. The proletarians cannot become masters of the productive forces of society except by abolishing their own previous mode of appropriation and thereby also every other previous mode of appropriation. They have nothing of their own to secure and to fortify; their mission is to destroy all previous securities for, and insurances of, individual property.

All previous historical movements were movements of minorities, or in the interest of minorities. The proletarian movement is the self-conscious, independent movement of the immense majority, in the interests of the immense majority. The proletariat, the lowest stratum of our present society, cannot stir, cannot raise itself up, without the whole superincumbent strata of official society being sprung into the air.

Though not in substance, yet in form, the struggle of the proletariat with the bourgeoisie is at first a national struggle. The proletariat of each country must, of course, first of all settle matters with its own bourgeoisie.

In depicting the most general phases of the development of the proletariat, we traced the more or less veiled civil war, raging within existing society, up to the point where that war breaks out into open revolution and where the violent overthrow of the bourgeoisie lays the foundation for the sway of the proletariat.

Hitherto, every form of society has been based, as we have already seen, on the antagonism of oppressing and oppressed classes. But in order to oppress a class, certain conditions must be assured to it under which it can, at least, continue its slavish existence. The serf, in the period of serfdom, raised himself to membership in the commune, just as the petty bourgeois, under the yoke of the feudal absolutism, managed to develop into a bourgeois. The modern laborer, on the contrary, instead of rising with the progress of industry, sinks deeper and deeper below t]

tions of existence of his own class. He becomes a pauper, and pauperism develops more rapidly than population and wealth. And here it becomes evident that the bourgeoisie is unfit any longer to be the ruling class in society and to impose its conditions of existence upon society as an overriding law. It is unfit to rule because it is incompetent to assure an existence to its slave within his slavery, because it cannot help letting him sink into such a state that it has to feed him, instead of being fed by him. Society can no longer live under this bourgeoisie; in other words, its existence is no longer compatible with society.

The essential condition for the existence and for the sway of the bourgeois class, is the formation and augmentation of capital; the condition for capital is wage labor. Wage labor rests exclusively on competition between the laborers. The advance of industry, whose involuntary promoter is the bourgeoisie, replaces the isolation of the laborers, due to competition, by their revolutionary combination, due to association. The development of modern industry, therefore, cuts from under its feet the very foundation on which the bourgeoisie produces and appropriates products. What the bourgeoisie, therefore, produces, above all, is its own gravediggers. Its fall and the victory of the proletariat are equally inevitable.

II. Proletarians and communists

In what relation do the communists stand to the proletarians as a whole?

The communists do not form a separate party opposed

to other working-class parties.

They have no interests separate and apart from those of the proletariat as a whole.

They do not set up any sectarian principles of their own, by which to shape and mold the proletarian movement.

The communists are distinguished from the other working-class parties by this only: (1) In the national struggles of the proletarians of the different countries, they point out and bring to the front the common interests of the entire proletariat, independently of all nationality. (2) In the various stages of development which the struggle of the working class against the bourgeoisie has to pass through, they always and everywhere represent the interests of the movement as a whole.

The communists, therefore, are on the one hand, practically, the most advanced and resolute section of the working-class parties of every country, that section which pushes forward all others; on the other hand, theoretically, they have over the great mass of the proletariat the advantage of clearly understanding the line of march, the conditions, and the ultimate general results of the proletarian movement.[21]

The immediate aim of the communists is the same as that of all the other proletarian parties: formation of the proletariat into a class, overthrow of the bourgeois supremacy, conquest of political power by the proletariat.

The theoretical conclusions of the communists are in no way based on ideas or principles that have been invented, or discovered, by this or that would-be universal reformer.

They merely express, in general terms, actual relations springing from an existing class struggle, from a historical movement going on under our very eyes. The abolition of existing property relations is not at all a distinctive feature of communism.

All property relations in the past have continually been subject to historical change consequent upon the change in historical conditions.

The French Revolution,[22] for example, abolished feudal property in favor of bourgeois property.

The distinguishing feature of communism is not the abolition of property generally, but the abolition of bourgeois property. But modern bourgeois private property is the final and most complete expression of the system of producing and appropriating products, that is based on class antagonisms, on the exploitation of the many by the few.

In this sense, the theory of the communists may be summed up in the single sentence: Abolition of private property.

We communists have been reproached with the desire of abolishing the right of personally acquiring property as the fruit of a man's own labor, which property is alleged to be the groundwork of all personal freedom, activity, and independence.

Hard-won, self-acquired, self-earned property! Do you mean the property of the petty artisan and of the small peasant, a form of property that preceded the bourgeois form? There is no need to abolish that; the development of industry has to a great extent already destroyed it and is still destroying it daily.

Or do you mean modern bourgeois private property?

But does wage labor create any property for the laborer? Not a bit. It creates capital, i.e., that kind of property which exploits wage labor and which cannot increase except upon conditions of begetting a new supply of wage labor for fresh exploitation. Property, in its present form, is based on the antagonism of capital and wage labor. Let us examine both sides of this antagonism.

To be a capitalist is to have not only a purely personal, but a social *status* in production. Capital is a collective product, and only by the united action of many members, nay, in the last resort, only by the united action of all members of society, can it be set in motion.

Capital is, therefore, not a personal, it is a social power.

When, therefore, capital is converted into common property, into the property of all members of society, personal property is not thereby transformed into social property. It is only the social character of the property that is changed. It loses its class character.

Let us now take wage labor.

The average price of wage labor is the minimum wage, i.e., that quantum of the means of subsistence which is absolutely requisite to keep the laborer in bare existence as a laborer. What, therefore, the wage-laborer appropriates by means of his labor merely suffices to prolong and reproduce a bare existence. We by no means intend to abolish this personal appropriation of the products of labor, an appropriation that is made for the maintenance and reproduction of human life and that leaves no surplus wherewith to command the labor of others. All that we want to do away with is the miserable character of this appropriation, under which the laborer lives merely to increase capital and is allowed to live only insofar as the interest of the ruling class requires it.

In bourgeois society, living labor is but a means to increase accumulated labor. In communist society, accumulated labor is but a means to widen, to enrich, to promote the existence of the laborer.

In bourgeois society, therefore, the past dominates the present; in communist society, the present dominates the past. In bourgeois society capital is independent and has individuality, while the living person is dependent and has no individuality.

And the abolition of this state of things is called by the bourgeois, abolition of individuality and freedom! And rightly so. The abolition of bourgeois individuality, bourgeois independence, and bourgeois freedom is undoubtedly aimed at.

By freedom is meant, under the present bourgeois conditions of production, free trade, free selling and buying.

But if selling and buying disappears, free selling and buying disappears also. This talk about free selling and buying, and all the other "brave words" of our bourgeoisie about freedom in general, have a meaning, if any, only in contrast with restricted selling and buying, with the fettered traders of the Middle Ages, but have no meaning when opposed to the communistic abolition of buying and selling, of the bourgeois conditions of production, and of the bourgeoisie itself.

You are horrified at our intending to do away with private property. But in your existing society, private property is already done away with for nine-tenths of the population; its existence for the few is solely due to its nonexistence in the hands of those nine-tenths. You reproach us, therefore, with intending to do away with a form of property, the necessary condition for whose existence is the nonexistence of any property for the immense majority of society.

In one word, you reproach us with intending to do away

with your property. Precisely so; that is just what we intend.

From the moment when labor can no longer be converted into capital, money, or rent, into a social power capable of being monopolized, i.e., from the moment when individual property can no longer be transformed into bourgeois property, into capital, from that moment, you say, individuality vanishes.

You must, therefore, confess that by "individual" you mean no other person than the bourgeois, than the middle-class owner of property. This person must, indeed, be swept out of the way and made impossible.

Communism deprives no man of the power to appropriate the products of society; all that it does is to deprive him of the power to subjugate the labor of others by means of such appropriation.

It has been objected that upon the abolition of private property all work will cease, and universal laziness will overtake us.

According to this, bourgeois society ought long ago to have gone to the dogs through sheer idleness; for those of its members who work, acquire nothing, and those who acquire anything, do not work. The whole of this objection is but another expression of the tautology: that there can no longer be any wage labor when there is no longer any capital.

All objections urged against the communistic mode of producing and appropriating material products have, in the same way, been urged against the communistic modes of producing and appropriating intellectual products. Just as, to the bourgeois, the disappearance of class property is the disappearance of production itself, so the disappearance of class culture is to him identical with the disappearance of all culture.

That culture, the loss of which he laments, is, for the enormous majority, a mere training to act as a machine.

But don't wrangle with us so long as you apply, to our intended abolition of bourgeois property, the standard of your bourgeois notions of freedom, culture, law, etc. Your very ideas are but the outgrowth of the conditions of your bourgeois production and bourgeois property, just as your jurisprudence is but the will of your class made into a law for all, a will whose essential character and direction are determined by the economic conditions of existence of your class.

The selfish misconception that induces you to transform into eternal laws of nature and of reason, the social forms springing from your present mode of production and form of property—historical relations that rise and disappear in the progress of production—this misconception you share with every ruling class that has preceded you. What you see clearly in the case of ancient property, what you admit in the case of feudal property, you are of course forbidden to admit in the case of your own bourgeois form of property.

Abolition of the family! Even the most radical flare up at this infamous proposal of the communists.

On what foundation is the present family, the bourgeois family, based? On capital, on private gain. In its completely developed form this family exists only among the bourgeoisie. But this state of things finds its complement in the practical absence of the family among the proletarians and in public prostitution.

The bourgeois family will vanish as a matter of course when its complement vanishes, and both will vanish with the vanishing of capital.

Do you charge us with wanting to stop the exploitation of children by their parents? To this crime we plead guilty.

But, you will say, we destroy the most hallowed of relations when we replace home education by social.

And your education! Is not that also social and determined by the social conditions under which you educate, by the intervention, direct or indirect, of society, by means of schools, etc.? The communists have not invented the intervention of society in education; they do but seek to alter the character of that intervention and to rescue education from the influence of the ruling class.

The bourgeois claptrap about the family and education, about the hallowed co-relation of parent and child, becomes all the more disgusting, the more, by the action of modern industry, all family ties among the proletarians are torn asunder, and their children transformed into simple articles of commerce and instruments of labor.

But you communists would introduce community of women, screams the whole bourgeoisie in chorus.

The bourgeois sees in his wife a mere instrument of production. He hears that the instruments of production are to be exploited in common and, naturally, can come to no other conclusion than that the lot of being common to all will likewise fall to the women.

He has not even a suspicion that the real point aimed at is to do away with the status of women as mere instruments of production.

For the rest, nothing is more ridiculous than the virtuous indignation of our bourgeois at the community of women which, they pretend, is to be openly and officially established by the communists. The communists have no need to introduce community of women; it has existed almost from time immemorial.

Our bourgeois, not content with having the wives and daughters of their proletarians at their disposal, not to speak of common prostitutes, take the greatest pleasure in seducing each other's wives.

Bourgeois marriage is in reality a system of wives in common and thus, at the most, what the communists might possibly be reproached with is that they desire to introduce, in substitution for a hypocritically concealed, an openly legalized community of women. For the rest, it is self-evident that the abolition of the present system of production must bring with it the abolition of the community of women springing from that system, i.e., of prostitution both public and private.

The communists are further reproached with desiring to abolish countries and nationality.

The working men have no country. We cannot take from them what they have not got. Since the proletariat must first of all acquire political supremacy, must rise to be the leading class of the nation, must constitute itself *the* nation, it is, so far, itself national, though not in the bourgeois sense of the word.

National differences and antagonisms between peoples are daily more and more vanishing, owing to the development of the bourgeoisie, to freedom of commerce, to the world market, to uniformity in the mode of production and in the conditions of life corresponding thereto.

The supremacy of the proletariat will cause them to vanish still faster. United action, of the leading civilized countries at least, is one of the first conditions for the emancipation of the proletariat.

In proportion as the exploitation of one individual by another is put an end to, the exploitation of one nation by another will also be put an end to. In proportion as the antagonism between classes within the nation vanishes, the hostility of one nation to another will come to an end.

The charges against communism made from a religious, a philosophical, and, generally, from an ideological standpoint are not deserving of serious examination.

Does it require deep intuition to comprehend that man's ideas, views, and conceptions, in one word, man's consciousness, changes with every change in the conditions of his material existence, in his social relations, and in his social life?

What else does the history of ideas prove, than that intellectual production changes its character in proportion as material production is changed? The ruling ideas of each age have ever been the ideas of its ruling class.

When people speak of ideas that revolutionize society, they do but express the fact that within the old society, the elements of a new one have been created, and that the dissolution of the old ideas keeps even pace with the dissolution of the old conditions of existence.

When the ancient world was in its last throes, the ancient religions were overcome by Christianity. When Christian ideas succumbed in the eighteenth century to rationalist ideas, feudal society fought its death battle with the then-revolutionary bourgeoisie. The ideas of religious liberty and freedom of conscience merely gave expression to the sway of free competition within the domain of knowledge.

"Undoubtedly," it will be said, "religious, moral, philosophical, and juridical ideas have been modified in the course of historical development. But religion, morality, philosophy, political science, and law constantly survived this change."

"There are, besides, eternal truths, such as Freedom, Justice, etc., that are common to all states of society. But communism abolishes eternal truths, it abolishes all religion and all morality, instead of constituting them on a new basis; it therefore acts in contradiction to all past historical experience."

What does this accusation reduce itself to? The history of all past society has consisted in the development of class antagonisms, antagonisms that assumed different forms at different epochs.

But whatever form they may have taken, one fact is common to all past ages, namely, the exploitation of one part of society by the other. No wonder, then, that the social consciousness of past ages, despite all the multiplicity and variety it displays, moves within certain common forms, or general ideas, which cannot completely vanish except with the total disappearance of class antagonisms.

The communist revolution is the most radical rupture with traditional property relations; no wonder that its development involves the most radical rupture with traditional ideas.

But let us have done with the bourgeois objections to communism.

We have seen above that the first step in the revolution by the working class is to raise the proletariat to the position of ruling class, to win the battle of democracy.

The proletariat will use its political supremacy to wrest, by degrees, all capital from the bourgeoisie, to centralize all instruments of production in the hands of the state, i.e., of the proletariat organized as the ruling class, and to increase the total of productive forces as rapidly as possible.

Of course, in the beginning, this cannot be effected except by means of despotic inroads on the rights of property and on the conditions of bourgeois production; by means of measures, therefore, which appear economically insufficient and untenable, but which, in the course of the movement, outstrip themselves, necessitate further inroads upon the old social order, and are unavoidable as a means of entirely revolutionizing the mode of production.

These measures will of course be different in different countries.

Nevertheless in the most advanced countries, the following will be pretty generally applicable.

1. Abolition of property in land and application of all rents of land to public purposes.

2. A heavy progressive or graduated income tax.

3. Abolition of all right of inheritance.

4. Confiscation of the property of all emigrants and rebels.

5. Centralization of credit in the hands of the state, by means of a national bank with state capital and an exclusive monopoly.

6. Centralization of the means of communication and transport in the hands of the state.

7. Extension of factories and instruments of production owned by the state; the bringing into cultivation of wastelands, and the improvement of the soil generally in accordance with a common plan.

8. Equal liability of all to labor. Establishment of industrial armies, especially for agriculture.

9. Combination of agriculture with manufacturing industries; gradual abolition of all the distinction between

town and country by a more equable distribution of the population over the country. 10. Free education for all children in public schools. Abolition of children's factory labor in its present form. Combination of education with industrial production, etc., etc.

When, in the course of development, class distinctions have disappeared, and all production has been concentrated in the hands of a vast association of the whole nation, the public power will lose its political character. Political power, properly so called, is merely the organized power of one class for oppressing another. If the proletariat during its contest with the bourgeoisie is compelled, by the force of circumstances, to organize itself as a class, if, by means of a revolution, it makes itself the ruling class, and, as such, sweeps away by force the old conditions of production, then it will, along with these conditions, have swept away the conditions for the existence of class antagonisms and of classes generally and will thereby have abolished its own supremacy as a class.

In place of the old bourgeois society, with its classes and class antagonisms, we shall have an association, in which the free development of each is the condition for the free development of all.

III. Socialist and communist literature

1. Reactionary socialism
a) Feudal socialism

Owing to their historical position, it became the vocation of the aristocracies of France and England to write pamphlets against modern bourgeois society. In the French revolution of July 1830, and in the English reform agitation,[23] these aristocracies again succumbed to the hateful upstart. Thenceforth, a serious political contest was altogether out of question. A literary battle alone remained possible. But even in the domain of literature the old cries of the restoration period* had become impossible.

In order to arouse sympathy, the aristocracy were obliged to lose sight, apparently, of their own interests and to formulate their indictment against the bourgeoisie in the interest of the exploited working class alone. Thus the aristocracy took their revenge by singing lampoons on their new master and whispering in his ears sinister prophecies of coming catastrophe.

In this way arose feudal socialism: half lamentation, half lampoon; half echo of the past, half menace of the future; at times, by its bitter, witty, and incisive criticism, striking the bourgeoisie to the very heart's core; but always ludicrous in its effect, through total incapacity to comprehend the march of modern history.

The aristocracy, in order to rally the people to them, waved the proletarian alms-bag in front for a banner. But the people, so often as it joined them, saw on their hindquarters the old feudal coats of arms and deserted with loud and irreverent laughter.

One section of the French Legitimists[25] and "Young England"[26] exhibited this spectacle.

In pointing out that their mode of exploitation was different to that of the bourgeoisie, the feudalists forget that

---

* Not the English Restoration 1660 to 1689, but the French Restoration 1814 to 1830.[24] [*Note by Engels to the English edition of 1888.*]

they exploited under circumstances and conditions that were quite different, and that are now antiquated. In showing that under their rule the modern proletariat never existed, they forget that the modern bourgeoisie is the necessary offspring of their own form of society.

For the rest, so little do they conceal the reactionary character of their criticism that their chief accusation against the bourgeoisie amounts to this, that under the bourgeois regime a class is being developed which is destined to cut up root and branch the old order of society.

What they upbraid the bourgeoisie with is not so much that it creates a proletariat, as that it creates a *revolutionary* proletariat.

In political practice, therefore, they join in all coercive measures against the working class; and in ordinary life, despite their highfalutin phrases, they stoop to pick up the golden apples dropped from the tree of industry and to barter truth, love, and honor for traffic in wool, beetroot-sugar, and potato spirits.*

As the parson has ever gone hand in hand with the landlord, so has clerical socialism with feudal socialism.

Nothing is easier than to give Christian asceticism a socialist tinge. Has not Christianity declaimed against private property, against marriage, against the state? Has it not preached in the place of these, charity and poverty,

---

* This applies chiefly to Germany where the landed aristocracy and squirearchy[27] have large portions of their estates cultivated for their own account by stewards and are, moreover, extensive beetroot-sugar manufacturers and distillers of potato spirits. The wealthier British aristocracy are, as yet, rather above that; but they, too, know how to make up for declining rents by lending their names to floaters of more or less shady joint-stock companies. [*Note by Engels to the English edition of 1888.*]

celibacy and mortification of the flesh, monastic life and Mother Church? Christian socialism is but the holy water with which the priest consecrates the heartburnings of the aristocrat.

b) Petty-bourgeois socialism

The feudal aristocracy was not the only class that was ruined by the bourgeoisie, not the only class whose conditions of existence pined and perished in the atmosphere of modern bourgeois society. The medieval burgesses and the small peasant proprietors were the precursors of the modern bourgeoisie. In those countries which are but little developed, industrially and commercially, these two classes still vegetate side by side with the rising bourgeoisie.

In countries where modern civilization has become fully developed, a new class of petty bourgeois has been formed, fluctuating between proletariat and bourgeoisie and ever renewing itself as a supplementary part of bourgeois society. The individual members of this class, however, are being constantly hurled down into the proletariat by the action of competition, and, as modern industry develops, they even see the moment approaching when they will completely disappear as an independent section of modern society, to be replaced, in manufactures, agriculture, and commerce, by overlookers, bailiffs, and shopmen.

In countries like France, where the peasants constitute far more than half of the population, it was natural that writers who sided with the proletariat against the bourgeoisie should use, in their criticism of the bourgeois regime, the standard of the peasant and petty bourgeois and from the standpoint of these intermediate classes should take up the cudgels for the working class. Thus arose petty-bourgeois socialism. Sismondi was the head of this school, not only in France but also in England.

This school of socialism dissected with great acuteness the contradictions in the conditions of modern production. It laid bare the hypocritical apologies of economists. It proved, incontrovertibly, the disastrous effects of machinery and division of labor; the concentration of capital and land in a few hands; overproduction and crises; it pointed out the inevitable ruin of the petty bourgeois and peasant, the misery of the proletariat, the anarchy in production, the crying inequalities in the distribution of wealth, the industrial war of extermination between nations, the dissolution of old moral bonds, of the old family relations, of the old nationalities.

In its positive aims, however, this form of socialism aspires either to restoring the old means of production and of exchange, and with them the old property relations and the old society, or to cramping the modern means of production and of exchange within the framework of the old property relations that have been, and were bound to be, exploded by those means. In either case, it is both reactionary and utopian.

Its last words are: corporate guilds for manufacture, patriarchal relations in agriculture.

Ultimately, when stubborn historical facts had dispersed all intoxicating effects of self-deception, this form of socialism ended in a miserable fit of the blues.

c) German, or 'true,' socialism

The socialist and communist literature of France, a literature that originated under the pressure of a bourgeoisie in power and that was the expression of the struggle against this power, was introduced into Germany at a time when the bourgeoisie, in that country, had just begun its contest with feudal absolutism.

German philosophers, would-be philosophers, and *beaux esprits* eagerly seized on this literature, only forgetting that when these writings immigrated from France into Germany, French social conditions had not immigrated along with them. In contact with German social conditions, this French literature lost all its immediate practical significance and assumed a purely literary aspect. Thus, to the German philosophers of the eighteenth century, the demands of the first French revolution were nothing more than the demands of "practical reason" in general, and the utterance of the will of the revolutionary French bourgeoisie signified in their eyes the laws of pure Will, of Will as it was bound to be, of true human Will generally.

The work of the German *literati* consisted solely in bringing the new French ideas into harmony with their ancient philosophical conscience, or rather, in annexing the French ideas without deserting their own philosophic point of view.

This annexation took place in the same way in which a foreign language is appropriated, namely, by translation.

It is well known how the monks wrote silly lives of Catholic saints *over* the manuscripts on which the classical works of ancient heathendom had been written. The German *literati* reversed this process with the profane French literature. They wrote their philosophical nonsense beneath the French original. For instance, beneath the French criticism of the economic functions of money, they wrote "Alienation of Humanity," and beneath the French criticism of the bourgeois state they wrote "Dethronement of the Category of the General," and so forth.

The introduction of these philosophical phrases at the back of the French historical criticisms they dubbed "Philosophy of Action," "True Socialism," "German Science of Socialism," "Philosophical Foundation of Socialism," and so on.

The French socialist and communist literature was thus completely emasculated. And, since it ceased in the hands of the German to express the struggle of one class with the other, he felt conscious of having overcome "French one-sidedness" and of representing, not true requirements, but the requirements of truth; not the interests of the proletariat, but the interests of human nature, of man in general, who belongs to no class, has no reality, who exists only in the misty realm of philosophical fantasy.

This German socialism, which took its schoolboy task so seriously and solemnly, and extolled its poor stock-in-trade in such mountebank fashion, meanwhile gradually lost its pedantic innocence.

The fight of the German and, especially, of the Prussian bourgeoisie against feudal aristocracy and absolute monarchy, in other words, the liberal movement, became more earnest.

By this, the long wished-for opportunity was offered to "true" socialism of confronting the political movement with the socialist demands, of hurling the traditional anathemas against liberalism, against representative government, against bourgeois competition, bourgeois freedom of the press, bourgeois legislation, bourgeois liberty and equality, and of preaching to the masses that they had nothing to gain, and everything to lose, by this bourgeois movement. German socialism forgot, in the nick of time, that the French criticism, whose silly echo it was, presupposed the existence of modern bourgeois society, with its corresponding economic conditions of existence, and the political constitution adapted thereto, the very things whose attainment was the object of the pending struggle in Germany.

To the absolute governments, with their following of parsons, professors, country squires, and officials, it served as a welcome scarecrow against the threatening bourgeoisie.

It was a sweet finish after the bitter pills of flogging and bullets with which these same governments, just at that time, dosed the German working-class risings.

While this "true" socialism thus served the governments as a weapon for fighting the German bourgeoisie, it, at the same time, directly represented a reactionary interest, the interest of the German philistines. In Germany the *petty-bourgeois* class, a relic of the sixteenth century, and since then constantly cropping up again under various forms, is the real social basis of the existing state of things.

To preserve this class is to preserve the existing state of things in Germany. The industrial and political supremacy of the bourgeoisie threatens it with certain destruction; on the one hand, from the concentration of capital; on the other, from the rise of a revolutionary proletariat. "True" socialism appeared to kill these two birds with one stone. It spread like an epidemic.

The robe of speculative cobwebs, embroidered with flowers of rhetoric, steeped in the dew of sickly sentiment, this transcendental robe in which the German socialists wrapped their sorry "eternal truths," all skin and bone, served to wonderfully increase the sale of their goods amongst such a public.

And on its part, German socialism recognized, more and more, its own calling as the bombastic representative of the petty-bourgeois philistine.

It proclaimed the German nation to be the model nation, and the German petty philistine to be the typical man. To every villainous meanness of this model man it gave a hidden, higher, socialistic interpretation, the exact contrary of its real character. It went to the extreme length of directly opposing the "brutally destructive" tendency of communism and of proclaiming its supreme and impartial contempt of all class struggles. With very few exceptions, all the so-called socialist and communist publications that now (1847) circulate in Germany belong to the domain of this foul and enervating literature.*

2. Conservative, or bourgeois, socialism

A part of the bourgeoisie is desirous of redressing social grievances, in order to secure the continued existence of bourgeois society.

To this section belong economists, philanthropists, humanitarians, improvers of the condition of the working class, organizers of charity, members of societies for the prevention of cruelty to animals, temperance fanatics, hole-and-corner reformers of every imaginable kind. This form of socialism has, moreover, been worked out into

---

* The revolutionary storm of 1848[28] swept away this whole shabby tendency and cured its protagonists of the desire to dabble further in socialism. The chief representative and classical type of this tendency is Herr Karl Grün. [*Note by Engels to the German edition of 1890.*]

complete systems.

We may cite Proudhon's *Philosophie de la Misère* as an example of this form.[29]

The socialistic bourgeois want all the advantages of modern social conditions without the struggles and dangers necessarily resulting therefrom. They desire the existing state of society minus its revolutionary and disintegrating elements. They wish for a bourgeoisie without a proletariat. The bourgeoisie naturally conceives the world in which it is supreme to be the best, and bourgeois socialism develops this comfortable conception into various more or less complete systems. In requiring the proletariat to carry out such a system, and thereby to march straightway into the social New Jerusalem,[30] it but requires in reality that the proletariat should remain within the bounds of existing society, but should cast away all its hateful ideas concerning the bourgeoisie.

A second and more practical, but less systematic, form of this socialism sought to depreciate every revolutionary movement in the eyes of the working class, by showing that no mere political reform, but only a change in the material conditions of existence, in economical relations, could be of any advantage to them. By changes in the material conditions of existence, this form of socialism, however, by no means understands abolition of the bourgeois relations of production, an abolition that can be effected only by a revolution, but administrative reforms, based on the continued existence of these relations; reforms, therefore, that in no respect affect the relations between capital and labor, but, at the best, lessen the cost, and simplify the administrative work, of bourgeois government.

Bourgeois socialism attains adequate expression when,

and only when, it becomes a mere figure of speech. Free trade: for the benefit of the working class. Protective duties: for the benefit of the working class. Prison reform: for the benefit of the working class. This is the last word and the only seriously meant word of bourgeois socialism.

It is summed up in the phrase: the bourgeois is a bourgeois—for the benefit of the working class.

3. Critical-utopian socialism and communism

We do not here refer to that literature which, in every great modern revolution, has always given voice to the demands of the proletariat, such as the writings of Babeuf[31] and others.

The first direct attempts of the proletariat to attain its own ends, made in times of universal excitement when feudal society was being overthrown, these attempts necessarily failed, owing to the then undeveloped state of the proletariat as well as to the absence of the economic conditions for its emancipation, conditions that had yet to be produced and could be produced by the impending bourgeois epoch alone. The revolutionary literature that accompanied these first movements of the proletariat had necessarily a reactionary character. It inculcated universal asceticism and social leveling in its crudest form.

The socialist and communist systems properly so called, those of Saint-Simon, Fourier, Owen, and others, spring into existence in the early undeveloped period, described above, of the struggle between proletariat and bourgeoisie (see Section I, "Bourgeois and proletarians").

The founders of these systems see, indeed, the class antagonisms, as well as the action of the decomposing elements, in the prevailing form of society. But the proletariat, as yet in its infancy, offers to them the spectacle of a class without any historical initiative or any independent political movement.

Since the development of class antagonism keeps even pace with the development of industry, the economic situation, as they find it, does not as yet offer to them the material conditions for the emancipation of the proletariat. They therefore search after a new social science, after new social laws that are to create these conditions.

Historical action is to yield to their personal inventive action, historically created conditions of emancipation to fantastic ones, and the gradual, spontaneous class organization of the proletariat to an organization of society specially contrived by these inventors. Future history resolves itself, in their eyes, into the propaganda and the practical carrying out of their social plans.

In the formation of their plans they are conscious of caring chiefly for the interests of the working class, as being the most suffering class. Only from the point of view of being the most suffering class does the proletariat exist for them.

The undeveloped state of the class struggle, as well as their own surroundings, causes socialists of this kind to consider themselves far superior to all class antagonisms. They want to improve the condition of every member of society, even that of the most favored. Hence, they habitually appeal to society at large, without distinction of class; nay, by preference, to the ruling class. For how can people, when once they understand their system, fail to see in it the best possible plan of the best possible state of society?

Hence they reject all political, and especially all revolutionary, action; they wish to attain their ends by peaceful means, and endeavor, by small experiments, necessarily doomed to failure, and by the force of example, to pave the way for the new social gospel.

Such fantastic pictures of future society, painted at a time when the proletariat is still in a very undeveloped state and has but a fantastic conception of its own position, correspond with the first instinctive yearnings of that class for a general reconstruction of society.

But these socialist and communist publications contain also a critical element. They attack every principle of existing society. Hence they are full of the most valuable materials for the enlightenment of the working class. The practical measures proposed in them—such as the abolition of the distinction between town and country, of the family, of the carrying on of industries for the account of private individuals, and of the wage system; the proclamation of social harmony, the conversion of the functions of the state into a mere superintendence of production, all these proposals point solely to the disappearance of class antagonisms which were, at that time, only just cropping up, and which, in these publications, are recognized in their earliest, indistinct, and undefined forms only. These proposals, therefore, are of a purely utopian character.

The significance of critical-utopian socialism and communism bears an inverse relation to historical development. In proportion as the modern class struggle develops and takes definite shape, this fantastic standing apart from the contest, these fantastic attacks on it, lose all practical value and all theoretical justification. Therefore, although the originators of these systems were, in many respects, revolutionary, their disciples have, in every case, formed mere reactionary sects. They hold fast by the original views of their masters, in opposition to the progressive historical development of the proletariat. They, therefore, endeavor, and that consistently, to deaden the class struggle and to reconcile the class antagonisms. They still dream of experimental realization of their social utopias, of founding isolated "*phalanstères*," of establishing "Home Colonies," or setting up a "Little Icaria"*—duodecimo editions of the New Jerusalem—and to realize all these castles in the air, they are compelled to appeal to the feelings and purses of the bourgeois. By degrees they sink into the category of the reactionary conservative socialists depicted above, differing from these only by more systematic pedantry and by their fanatical and superstitious belief in the miraculous effects of their social science.

They, therefore, violently oppose all political action on the part of the working class; such action, according to them, can only result from blind unbelief in the new gospel.

The Owenites in England, and the Fourierists in France, respectively, oppose the Chartists[32] and the *Réformistes*.[33]

---

* *Phalanstères* were socialist colonies on the plan of Charles Fourier; *Icaria* was the name given by Cabet to his utopia and, later on, to his American communist colony. [*Note by Engels to the English edition of 1888.*]

"Home colonies" were what Owen called his communist model societies. *Phalanstères* was the name of the public palaces planned by Fourier. *Icaria* was the name given to the utopian land of fancy, whose communist institutions Cabet portrayed. [*Note by Engels to the German edition of 1890.*]

IV. Position of the communists in relation to the various existing opposition parties ·

Section II has made clear the relations of the communists to the existing working-class parties, such as the Chartists in England and the Agrarian Reformers in America.

The communists fight for the attainment of the immediate aims, for the enforcement of the momentary interests of the working class; but in the movement of the present, they also represent and take care of the future of that movement. In France the communists ally themselves with the Social Democrats,* against the conservative and radical bourgeoisie, reserving, however, the right to take up a critical position in regard to phrases and illusions traditionally handed down from the great revolution.

In Switzerland they support the Radicals, without losing sight of the fact that this party consists of antagonistic elements, partly of democratic socialists, in the French sense, partly of radical bourgeois.

In Poland they support the party that insists on an agrarian revolution as the prime condition for national emancipation, that party which fomented the insurrection of Cracow in 1846.[34]

---

* The party then represented in Parliament by Ledru-Rollin, in literature by Louis Blanc, in the daily press by the *Réforme*. The name of Social Democracy signified, with these its inventors, a section of the democratic or republican party more or less tinged with socialism. [*Note by Engels to the English edition of 1888.*]

The party in France which at that time called itself Socialist-Democratic was represented in political life by Ledru-Rolin and in literature by Louis Blanc; thus it differed immeasurably from present-day German Social Democracy. [*Note by Engels to the German edition of 1890.*]

In Germany they fight with the bourgeoisie whenever it acts in a revolutionary way, against the absolute monarchy, the feudal squirearchy, and the petty bourgeoisie.

But they never cease, for a single instant, to instill into the working class the clearest possible recognition of the hostile antagonism between bourgeoisie and proletariat, in order that the German workers may straightway use, as so many weapons against the bourgeoisie, the social and political conditions that the bourgeoisie must necessarily introduce along with its supremacy, and in order that, after the fall of the reactionary classes in Germany, the fight against the bourgeoisie itself may immediately begin.

The communists turn their attention chiefly to Germany, because that country is on the eve of a bourgeois revolution that is bound to be carried out under more advanced conditions of European civilization, and with a much more developed proletariat, than that of England was in the seventeenth and of France in the eighteenth century, and because the bourgeois revolution in Germany will be but the prelude to an immediately following proletarian revolution.

In short, the communists everywhere support every revolutionary movement against the existing social and political order of things.

In all these movements they bring to the front, as the leading question in each, the property question, no matter what its degree of development at the time.

Finally, they labor everywhere for the union and agreement of the democratic parties of all countries.

The communists disdain to conceal their views and aims. They openly declare that their ends can be attained only by the forcible overthrow of all existing social conditions.

Let the ruling classes tremble at a communistic revolution. The proletarians have nothing to lose but their chains. They have a world to win.

Workingmen of all countries, unite!

NOTES

1. The Communist International, or Comintern, was founded under the leadership of V.I. Lenin and the Bolshevik Party in 1919, as the world organization of the communist workers movement. In the years following Lenin's death the Comintern was transformed into a tool for the counterrevolutionary policies of the privileged caste headed by Joseph Stalin. Leon Trotsky was the central leader of those in the Bolshevik and Comintern leadership who waged a political fight to continue Lenin's proletarian internationalist course.

The People's Front refers to the Stalinists' policy of subordinating the political independence and program of workers parties and the Communist International to collaboration with liberal capitalist parties, in pursuit of the nationalist and diplomatic interests of the bureaucratic caste in the USSR.

2. Eduard Bernstein (1850–1932) was the leading exponent of revisionism in the German Social Democratic Party (SPD), rejecting class struggle and revolution in favor of a gradual reform of capitalism and collaboration with capitalist parties. Karl Kautsky (1854–1938) was a leading Marxist within the Second International until World War I, when he became a centrist apologist for the chauvinist SPD majority; he was an opponent of the October 1917 revolution in Russia and the Bolshevik led workers and peasants republic.

3. Léon Blum (1872–1950) was head of the French Socialist Party and prime minister of the first People's Front government of 1936–37. Camille Chautemps (1885–1963), leader of the Radical Socialists, a liberal capitalist party, was French prime minister in 1930, 1933–34, and 1937–38. Francisco Largo Caballero (1869–1946) was leader of the Spanish Socialist Party and prime minister from September 1936 to May 1937. He was succeeded by Juan Negrín (1889–1956), the last prime minister of the Spanish Republic prior to the victory of the forces led by Gen. Francisco Franco in 1939.

4. Bonapartism originates in a period of social crisis and strives to concentrate executive power in the hands of a "strong man." The Bonapartist leader presents himself as standing above contending class forces, with the aim of maintaining the power of the dominant social class or layer. The term refers to the way in which this balancing between class forces was carried out in the wake of the French Revolution by Napoleon Bonaparte (from 1799 through his final defeat by a coalition of European monarchies in 1815), and then in the aftermath of the 1848–49 revolutions in France by Napoleon's nephew Louis Bonaparte (from a December 1851 coup to the fall of his regime in 1870 at the close of the Franco-Prussian War).

Socialism in one country—As an ideological rationalization for abandoning Lenin's proletarian internationalist course, Stalin in 1924 introduced the view that socialism could be achieved inside the borders of a single country. This conception was later incorporated into the program and tactics of the Comintern, and used to justify the conversion of Communist parties around the world into pawns of the Kremlin's foreign policy. See Leon Trotsky, *The Third International After Lenin* (New York: Pathfinder, 1970).

5. The Second International—founded in 1889, with the participation of Frederick Engels, as an international association of workers parties. It collapsed at the outbreak of World War I when most of the leaderships of its largest parties backed their respective bourgeoisies in the slaughter. It was reestablished in 1923 as the reformist Labor and Socialist International.

6. In 1848, struggles took place throughout Europe for democratic rights, national unification and independence, and constitutional reforms. The emerging working classes and plebeian forces fought to bring their demands and social weight to bear on the outcome of these bourgeois democratic revolutions. The Paris Commune of 1871 was the first attempt to establish a revolutionary government of the toilers. The working people of Paris held the city and administered it from March 18 until May 28, when their resistance was crushed by the French bourgeoisie, working in league with the occupying army of Prussia. In the ensuing terror more than seventeen thousand working people of Paris were massacred.

7. The Fourth International was founded in 1938 under Trotsky's guidance to regroup revolutionists willing to fight to advance the communist policies defended by V.I. Lenin, and who refused to capitulate to the counterrevolutionary politics and police state terrorism that, by the early 1930s, had become consolidated in the Stalinized government and party in the Soviet Union, and in the Comintern.

8. The Communist League—the first international communist organization of the proletariat—was founded in London in June 1847 by revolutionary workers' leaders from Germany and across Europe; it existed until 1852. Its second congress, held in November–December 1847, asked Marx and Engels to draft its program, which became the Communist Manifesto. See Engels, "On the History of the Communist League," in Marx and Engels, *Collected Works*, vol. 26, pp. 312–30 (New York: International Publishers, 1975).

9. This refers to the February revolution of 1848 in France.

10. The *Red Republican*—a Chartist weekly published in London by George Julian Harney from June to November 1850. It carried an abridged version of the Manifesto in nos. 21–24, November 1850.

11. The reference is to the uprising of the Paris workers of June

23–26, 1848, which was suppressed by the French bourgeoisie with extreme brutality. This insurrection was the first great civil war between the proletariat and the bourgeoisie.

12. *Le Socialiste* was a weekly French language newspaper published in New York from October 1871 to May 1873. It was an organ of the French sections of the North American Federation of the First International; after the Hague congress of 1872 it broke away from the International. The French translation of the Manifesto referred to in the text was published in *Le Socialiste* between January and March 1872.

13. In Marx and Engels, *Collected Works*, vol. 22, pp. 307–60.

14. The Cologne Communist trial (October 4–November 12, 1852)—a frame up trial of eleven members of the Communist League staged by the Prussian government. Charged with high treason on the basis of forged documents and false evidence, seven of the accused were sentenced to terms of imprisonment in a fortress varying from three to six years. The provocations of the Prussian police state against the international working class movement were exposed by Marx and Engels. See Engels, "The Late Trial at Cologne" and Marx, "Revelations Concerning the Communist Trial in Cologne," in Marx and Engels, *Collected Works*, vol. 11, pp. 388–93 and 395–457.

15. See Marx, "General Rules of the International Working Men's Association," in *Collected Works*, vol. 23, pp. 3–8.

16. This refers to the June insurrection of 1848 in Paris.

17. This preface was written by Engels on May 1, 1890, the day when, in accordance with the decision of the Paris congress of the Second International (July 1889), mass demonstrations, strikes, and meetings were held in a number of countries of Europe and America. From that time onwards the first of May began to be celebrated annually by the workers of all countries as the day of international solidarity of the proletariat.

18. Prince Von Metternich (1773–1859), Austrian chancellor 1821–48, and leading figure in the reactionary Holy Alliance from the end of the Napoleonic wars in 1815 to the revolution of 1848. François Guizot (1787–1874) directed the French government from 1840 to 1848.

19. The crusades were the military colonialist expeditions to the East by the western European big feudal lords, knights, and Italian merchants in the eleventh to the thirteenth centuries under the guise of recovering shrines in Jerusalem and other "holy places" from the Muslims. The crusades were inspired and justified by the Catholic church hierarchy, which was striving for world domination, while the knights made up the main fighting force. Peasants who sought liberation from the feudal yoke also took part in the crusades. The crusaders resorted to plunder and violence against both the Muslim and Christian population of the countries through which they marched. The objects of their predatory aspirations were not only the Muslim states in Syria, Palestine, Egypt, and Tunisia, but the Orthodox Byzantine Empire. Their conquests in the eastern Mediterranean area were, however, not lasting, and soon they were recovered by the Muslims.

20. In their later works, Marx and Engels used the more exact terms "the value of labor power" and "the price of labor power" introduced by Marx instead of "the value of labor" and "the price of labor." (See in this connection Engels's introduction to Marx's "Wage Labor and Capital," in *Collected Works*, vol. 27, pp. 194–201.)

21. In September 1847, as Marx and Engels were working on drafts of what would soon become the program of the Communist League, Engels developed the central points summarized in this section of the Manifesto in a reply to several attacks on communism by a liberal petty bourgeois journalist named Karl Heinzen. Heinzen, Engels wrote, "imagines communism is a certain *doctrine* which proceeds from a definite theoretical principle at its *core* and draws further conclusions from that. Herr Heinzen is very much mistaken. Communism is not a doctrine but a *movement*; it proceeds not from principles but from *facts*. The Communists do not base themselves on this or that philosophy as their point of departure but on the whole course of previous history and specifically its actual results in the civilized countries at the present time. Communism has followed from large scale industry and its consequences, from the establishment of the world market, of the concomitant uninhibited competition, from the ever more violent and more universal trade crises, which have already become full fledged crises of the world market, from the creation of the proletariat and the concentration of capital, from the ensuing class struggle between proletariat and bourgeoisie. Communism, insofar as it is a theory, is the theoretical expression of the position of the proletariat in this struggle and the theoretical summation of the conditions for liberation of the proletariat." See "The Communists and Karl Heinzen" in Marx and Engels, *Collected Works*, vol. 6, pp. 291–306.

22. This refers to the French bourgeois revolution at the end of the eighteenth century.

23. The English reform agitation refers to the movement for a reform of the electoral law which, under pressure from the people, was passed by the House of Commons in 1831 and was finally endorsed by the House of Lords in June 1832. This reform was directed against the monopoly rule of the landed and financial aristocracy and opened the way to Parliament for the representatives of the industrial bourgeoisie. The proletariat and the petty bourgeoisie, who were the main force in the struggle for the reform, were deceived by the liberal bourgeoisie and were not granted electoral rights.

24. The Restoration of 1660–89—the second period of the rule in England of the Stuart dynasty, which was overthrown by the English bourgeois revolution of the seventeenth century.

The Restoration of 1814–30—a period of the second reign in

France of the Bourbon dynasty. The reactionary regime of the Bourbons which supported the interests of the nobles and the clericals was overthrown by the July revolution of 1830.

25. The Legitimists were the adherents of the "legitimate" Bourbon dynasty overthrown in 1830, which represented the interests of the big landed nobility. In their struggle against the reigning Orleans dynasty (1830–48), which relied on the financial aristocracy and big bourgeoisie, a section of the Legitimists resorted to social demagogy and projected themselves as defenders of the working people against exploitation by the bourgeoisie.

26. "Young England"—a group of British Conservatives—men of politics and literature—was formed in the early 1840s. While expressing the dissatisfaction of the landed aristocracy with the growing economic and political might of the bourgeoisie, the "Young England" leaders resorted to demagogic ruses in order to subjugate the working class to their influence and to turn it into a tool in their struggle against the bourgeoisie.

27. Squirearchy or Junkerdom means, in the narrow sense, the landed nobility in East Prussia; in the broad sense this means a class of German landowners.

28. This refers to the 1848–49 bourgeois democratic revolution in Germany.

29. Pierre Joseph Proudhon (1809–1865) was a utopian socialist who called for a society based on fair exchange between producers and replacement of the state by a network of workshops. His book *The Philosophy of Poverty* was answered by Marx in *The Poverty of Philosophy.*

30. New Jerusalem was a synonym for paradise according to the Christian tradition.

31. François Noel (Gracchus) Babeuf (1760–1797) was a leader of a revolutionary plebeian current in France during the period of the Thermidorian reaction who advocated a form of utopian communism. He was executed, together with a number of his followers, by the government.

32. The Chartists were the first mass working class political movement in Britain. From the 1830s to the mid 1850s they campaigned for universal suffrage and other political and social demands in the interests of the exploited producers, as put forward in the People's Charter.

33. This refers to petty bourgeois republican democrats and petty bourgeois socialists who were adherents of *La Réforme*, a daily newspaper published in Paris from 1843 to 1850. They came out for a republic and democratic and social reforms.

34. In February 1846 preparations were made for an insurrection throughout the Polish territories with the aim of achieving national liberation. Polish revolutionary democrats (Dabrowski and others) were its main inspirers. However, as a result of the betrayal by a section of the Polish gentry and the arrest of the leaders of the insurrection by the Prussian police, only isolated risings broke out. Only in Cracow, which from 1815 onwards was jointly controlled by Austria, Russia, and Prussia, did the insurgents gain a victory on February 22 and establish a national government, which issued a manifesto repealing obligatory services to the feudal lords. The Cracow uprising was crushed early in March 1846. In November 1846 Austria, Prussia, and Russia signed a treaty according to which Cracow was annexed to the Austrian empire.

INDEX

FROM PATHFINDER

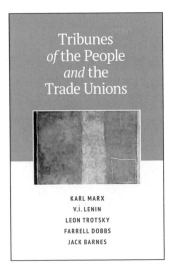

Tribunes of the People and the Trade Unions

KARL MARX, V.I. LENIN, LEON TROTSKY, FARRELL DOBBS, JACK BARNES

A tribune of the people uses every example of capitalist oppression to explain why working people, in class battles, will lay the foundations of a socialist world of human solidarity. Features 1940 unfinished article by Trotsky on trade unions. $12. Also in Spanish.

Malcolm X, Black Liberation, and the Road to Workers Power

JACK BARNES

The conquest of state power by a class-conscious vanguard of the working class is the mightiest weapon working people can wield against not only racism and Black oppression but every form of human degradation inherited from class society. $20. Also in Spanish, French, Farsi, Arabic, and Greek.

The Turn to Industry: Forging a Proletarian Party

JACK BARNES

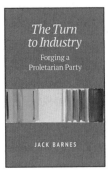

About the working-class program, composition, and course of conduct of the only kind of party worthy of the name "revolutionary" in the imperialist epoch. One that can recognize the most revolutionary fact of this epoch—the worth of working people, and our power to change society when we organize and act against the capitalist class in all its economic, social, and political forms. About building such a party in the US and in other capitalist countries around the world. $15. Also in Spanish.

Are They Rich Because They're Smart?

Class, Privilege, and Learning under Capitalism

JACK BARNES

Exposes the self-serving rationalizations by well-paid middle-class layers that their intelligence and schooling equip them to "regulate" workers' lives. Includes "Capitalism, the Working Class, and the Transformation of Learning." $10. Also in Spanish, French, and Farsi.

Is Socialist Revolution in the US Possible?

A Necessary Debate among Working People

MARY-ALICE WATERS

Fighting for a society only working people can create, it is our own capacities we will discover. And along that course we will answer the question posed here with a resounding "Yes." Possible but not inevitable. That depends on us. $7. Also in Spanish, French, and Farsi.

The Clintons' Anti-Working-Class Record

Why Washington Fears Working People

JACK BARNES

What working people need to know about the profit-driven course of Democrats and Republicans alike since the White House of William and Hillary Clinton in the 1990s. And the political awakening of workers seeking to understand and resist the capitalist rulers' assaults. $10. Also in Spanish, French, Farsi, and Greek.

WWW.PATHFINDERPRESS.COM

The Teamster series

FARRELL DOBBS

From the 1934 strikes that won union recognition to the fight by class-conscious workers to oppose Washington's objectives in World War II.

"These books are not 'manuals' or handbooks. They are the record of a concrete experience in the class struggle— one that can be studied and absorbed by class-conscious workers and farmers who find themselves in the midst of other struggles, at other times, in other conditions, speaking many different languages." —Jack Barnes.
$16 each. Also in Spanish. *Teamster Rebellion* is available in French, Farsi, and Greek.

In Defense of the US Working Class

MARY-ALICE WATERS

Hillary Clinton calls them "deplorables" who inhabit the "backward" regions between New York and San Francisco. But tens of thousands of teachers and other school employees in West Virginia set an example in 2018 with the most powerful labor action in decades. And working people across Florida mobilized and won restoration of voting rights to more than one million former prisoners. They fought for dignity and respect for themselves, their families, and for all working people. $7. Also in Spanish, French, and Farsi.

"It's the Poor Who Face the Savagery of the US 'Justice' System"

The Cuban Five Talk about Their Lives within the US Working Class

How US cops, courts, and prisons work as "an enormous machine for grinding people up." Five Cuban revolutionaries framed up and held in US jails for 16 years explain the human devastation of capitalist "justice"—and how socialist Cuba is different. $10. Also in Spanish, Farsi, and Greek.

ALSO BY KARL MARX AND FREDERICK ENGELS

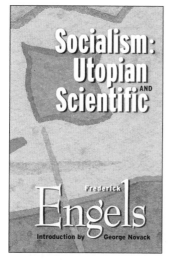

Socialism: Utopian and Scientific

FREDERICK ENGELS

"To make man the master of his own form of social organization—to make him free—is the historical mission of the modern proletariat," writes Engels. Here socialism is placed on a scientific foundation, the product of the lawful operations of capitalism itself and the struggles of the working class. $10. Also in Farsi.

Capital

KARL MARX

Marx explains the workings of the capitalist system and how it produces the insoluble contradictions that breed class struggle. He demonstrates the inevitability of the revolutionary transformation of society into one ruled for the first time by the producing majority: the working class. Volume 1, $18; volume 2, $18; volume 3, $18. Also in Spanish.

Origin of the Family, Private Property, and the State

FREDERICK ENGELS

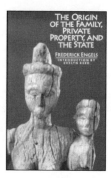

How the emergence of class-divided society gave rise to repressive state bodies and family structures that protect the property of the ruling layers and enable them to pass along wealth and privilege. Engels discusses the consequences for working people of these class institutions—from their original forms to their modern versions. $15. Also in Farsi.

WWW.PATHFINDERPRESS.COM

CUBA'S SOCIALIST REVOLUTION

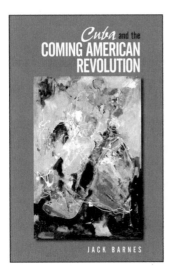

Cuba and the Coming American Revolution

JACK BARNES

This is a book about the struggles of working people in the imperialist heartland, the youth attracted to them, and the example set by the Cuban people that revolution is not only necessary—it can be made. It is about the class struggle in the US, where the revolutionary capacities of workers and farmers are today as utterly discounted by the ruling powers as were those of the Cuban toilers. And just as wrongly. $10. Also in Spanish, French, and Farsi.

Women in Cuba: The Making of a Revolution within the Revolution

VILMA ESPÍN, ASELA DE LOS SANTOS, YOLANDA FERRER

The integration of women into the ranks and leadership of the Cuban Revolution was inseparably intertwined with the proletarian course of the revolution from its very first actions. This is the story of that revolution and how it transformed the women and men who made it. $17. Also in Spanish and Greek.

The First and Second Declarations of Havana

Nowhere are the questions of revolutionary strategy that today confront men and women on the front lines of struggles in the Americas addressed with greater truthfulness and clarity than in these uncompromising indictments of imperialist plunder and "the exploitation of man by man." Adopted by million-strong assemblies of the Cuban people in 1960 and 1962. $10. Also in Spanish, French, Farsi, Arabic, and Greek.

Cuba and Angola: The War for Freedom

HARRY VILLEGAS ("POMBO")

The story of Cuba's unparalleled contribution to the fight to free Africa from the scourge of apartheid. And how, in the doing, Cuba's socialist revolution was strengthened. $10. Also in Spanish.

Companion volume

Cuba and Angola

Fighting for Africa's Freedom and Our Own

FIDEL CASTRO, RAÚL CASTRO, NELSON MANDELA, OTHERS

$12. Also in Spanish.

Our History Is Still Being Written

The Story of Three Chinese Cuban Generals in the Cuban Revolution

ARMANDO CHOY, GUSTAVO CHUI, MOISÉS SÍO WONG, MARY-ALICE WATERS

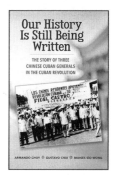

"What ~~was~~ the key measure to uproot discrimination against Chinese and blacks in Cuba? It was the socialist revolution itself." New edition sheds light on Chinese Cubans' involvement in Cuba's internationalist course, including in Africa and Latin America. $15. Also in Spanish, French, Farsi, and Chinese.

How Far We Slaves Have Come!

South Africa and Cuba in Today's World

NELSON MANDELA, FIDEL CASTRO

Cuban internationalists "made a contribution to African independence, freedom, and justice, unparalleled for its principles and selfless character," said Nelson Mandela, speaking in Cuba in July 1991 alongside Fidel Castro. Here are their speeches on the victory by Cuban, Angolan, and Namibian combatants over the US-backed South African army that had invaded Angola. $7. Also in Spanish and Farsi.

WWW.PATHFINDERPRESS.COM

New International

A MAGAZINE OF MARXIST POLITICS AND THEORY

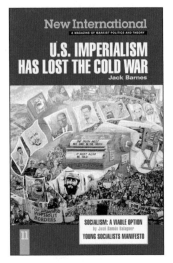

U.S. Imperialism Has Lost the Cold War

JACK BARNES

The collapse of regimes across Eastern Europe and the USSR claiming to be communist did not mean workers and farmers there had been defeated. In today's sharpening capitalist conflicts and wars, these toilers have joined working people the world over in the class struggle against exploitation. In *New International* no. 11. $14. Also in Spanish, French, Farsi, and Greek.

In Defense of Land and Labor

"All progress in capitalist agriculture is progress in the art, not only of robbing the worker, but of robbing the soil.... Capitalist production, therefore, only develops by simultaneously undermining the original sources of all wealth— the soil and the worker."—*Karl Marx, 1867*

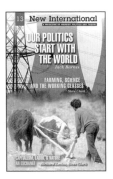

FOUR ARTICLES

IN *NEW INTERNATIONAL* NO. 13

• **Our Politics Start with the World**
  JACK BARNES

• **Farming, Science, and the Working Classes**
  STEVE CLARK

• **Capitalism, Labor, and the Transformation of Nature: An Exchange**
  RICHARD LEVINS, STEVE CLARK

IN *NEW INTERNATIONAL* NO. 14

• **The Stewardship of Nature Also Falls to the Working Class**
  JACK BARNES, STEVE CLARK, MARY-ALICE WATERS

$14 each issue

WOMEN'S LIBERATION AND SOCIALISM

Cosmetics, Fashions, and the Exploitation of Women
Joseph Hansen, Evelyn Reed, Mary-Alice Waters

How big business plays on women's second-class status in class society and what Reed calls "capitalist social compulsion" to market cosmetics and rake in profits. And how the entry of millions of women into the workforce has irreversibly changed relations between women and men—for the better. $12. Also in Spanish and Farsi.

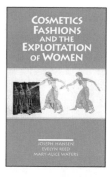

Woman's Evolution
From Matriarchal Clan to Patriarchal Family
Evelyn Reed

Assesses women's leading and still largely unknown contributions to the development of human civilization and refutes the myth that women have always been subordinate to men. "Certain to become a classic text in women's history."
—*Publishers Weekly.* $25. Also in Farsi.

Abortion Is a Woman's Right!
Pat Grogan, Evelyn Reed

Why abortion rights are central not only to the fight for the full emancipation of women, but to forging a united and fighting labor movement. $5. Also in Spanish.

Communist Continuity and the Fight for Women's Liberation
Documents of the Socialist Workers Party, 1971–86

How did the oppression of women begin? Who benefits? What social forces have the power to end women's second-class status? 3 volumes, edited with preface by Mary-Alice Waters. $12

WWW.PATHFINDERPRESS.COM

REVOLUTIONARY LEADERS IN THEIR OWN WORDS

Malcolm X Talks to Young People

"The young generation of whites, Blacks, browns, whatever else there is—you're living at a time of revolution," Malcolm said in December 1964. "And I for one will join in with anyone, I don't care what color you are, as long as you want to change this miserable condition that exists on this earth." $12. Also in Spanish, French, Farsi, and Greek.

Episodes of the Cuban Revolutionary War, 1956–58

ERNESTO CHE GUEVARA

A firsthand account of political events and military campaigns that culminated in the January 1959 popular insurrection that overthrew the US-backed dictatorship in Cuba. With clarity and humor, Guevara describes his own political education. He explains how the struggle transformed the men and women of the Rebel Army and July 26 Movement, opening the door to the first socialist revolution in the Americas. $23

The Jewish Question

A Marxist Interpretation

ABRAM LEON

Traces the historical rationalizations of anti-Semitism to the fact that Jews became a "people-class" of merchants and moneylenders in the centuries before industrial capitalism. And how, in times of crisis, capitalists mobilize renewed Jew-hatred to incite reactionary forces and disorient working people about the true source of their impoverishment. $15. Also in Greek.

Maurice Bishop Speaks

The Grenada Revolution and Its Overthrow, 1979–83

The triumph of the 1979 revolution in the Caribbean island of Grenada under the leadership of Maurice Bishop gave hope to millions throughout the Americas. Invaluable lessons from the workers and farmers government destroyed by a Stalinist-led coup in 1983. $20

Aldabonazo

Inside the Cuban Revolutionary Underground, 1952–58

ARMANDO HART

In this account by a historic leader of the Cuban Revolution, we meet men and women who led the urban underground in the fight against the brutal US-backed tyranny in the 1950s. Together with their comrades-in-arms in the Rebel Army, they not only overthrew the dictatorship. Their revolutionary actions and example worldwide changed the history of the 20th century—and of the twenty-first. $20. Also in Spanish.

Thomas Sankara Speaks

The Burkina Faso Revolution, 1983–87

Under Sankara's guidance, Burkina Faso's revolutionary government led peasants, workers, women, and youth to expand literacy; to sink wells, plant trees, erect housing; to combat women's oppression; to carry out land reform; to join others in Africa and worldwide to free themselves from the imperialist yoke. $20. Also in French.

WWW.PATHFINDERPRESS.COM

THE RUSSIAN REVOLUTION

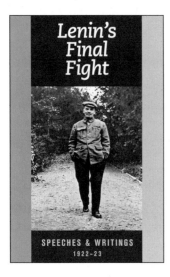

Lenin's Final Fight

Speeches and Writings, 1922–23

V.I. LENIN

In 1922 and 1923, V.I. Lenin, central leader of the world's first socialist revolution, waged what was to be his last political battle—one that was lost following his death. At stake was whether that revolution, and the international communist movement it led, would remain on the revolutionary proletarian course that had brought workers and peasants to power in October 1917. $17. Also in Spanish, Farsi, and Greek.

In Defense of Marxism

Against the Petty-Bourgeois Opposition in the Socialist Workers Party

LEON TROTSKY

Writing in 1939–40, Leon Trotsky replies to those in the revolutionary workers movement beating a retreat from defense of the Soviet Union in face of the looming imperialist assault. Why only a party that fights to bring growing numbers of workers into its ranks and leadership can steer a steady revolutionary course. $17. Also in Spanish.

Women and the Family

LEON TROTSKY

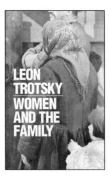

How the October 1917 Russian Revolution, the first victorious socialist revolution, opened the door to new possibilities in the fight for women's liberation. $10